ARE YOU READY FOR THE END OF TIME?

J. C. RYLE

ARE YOU READY FOR THE END OF TIME?

UNDERSTANDING FUTURE EVENTS FROM PROPHETIC PASSAGES OF THE BIBLE

J. C. RYLE

CHRISTIAN FOCUS

© Christian Focus Publications

ISBN 1-85792-747-8
ISBN 978-1-85792-747-7

10 9 8 7 6 5 4 3 2 1

Previously published as
Coming Events And Present Duties,
and *Prophecy.*

This edition published in 2001,
reprinted 2006
in the
Christian Heritage Imprint
by
Christian Focus Publications Ltd.
Geanies House, Fearn, Ross-shire,
IV20 1TW, Scotland, Great Britain.

www.christianfocus.com

Cover design by Alister MacInnes

Printed and bound by J H Haynes

Contents

FOREWORD

The reader of this volume will probably observe that some of the thoughts and ideas are occasionally repeated. They will kindly remember that this arises from the sermons which comprise it having been delivered at different places, and at long intervals. I have thought it best and wisest, for many reasons, to reprint them without alteration.

J C Ryle
Stradbroke Vicarage, August 1867

PREFACE

The volume now in the reader's hands requires a few introductory words of explanation.

It contains little that is entirely new. It consists of eight sermons, delivered on public occasions, at various intervals during my ministry, and afterwards published in the form of tracts. Of these sermons, one or two have perhaps obtained a greater circulation than they deserved, while one or two, in my humble judgment of more real worth, have received comparatively little notice. They are now brought together in their present form, for the convenience of those who wish to have a manual of my views of prophecy in a compact state.

At the very outset I warn the reader of these pages that he will find here nothing deep or abstruse. I have purposely avoided everything that can be called speculative or conjectural. I have strictly confined myself to a few great prophetic principles, which appear to me written as it were with a sunbeam. I have not attempted to expound such portions of God's Word as Ezekiel's temple, or symbolical visions of Revelation. I have not ventured to fix any dates. I have not tried to settle the precise order or manner in which predictions of things to come are to be fulfilled. There is nothing I dislike so much in prophetical inquiry as dogmatism or positiveness. Much of the discredit which has fallen on prophetical study has arisen from the fact that many students instead of expounding prophecy have turned prophets themselves.

If any one asks me what my prophetical opinions are, I am quite ready to give him an answer. Cautious and doubtful as I feel on some points, there are certain great principles about which I have fully made up my mind. I have held by them firmly for many years, and have never had my opinion shaken about them. I have lived in the belief of them for more than a third of a century, and in the belief of them I hope to die. The older I grow, the more do I feel convinced of their truth, and the more satisfied am I that no other principles can explain the state of the Church and the world.

One thing only I wish to premise, before making my statement. The reader must distinctly understand that I do not put forth my prophetical views as articles of faith, but only as my private opinions. I do not say that nobody can be saved who does not agree with me about prophecy. I am not infallible. I am very sensible that holier and better men than myself do not see these subjects with my eyes, and think me utterly mistaken. I condemn nobody; I judge nobody. I only ask liberty to hold and state distinctly my own views. The day will decide who is right. It is the new heart, and faith in Christ's blood, which are absolutely necessary to salvation. The man who knows these two things experimentally may be wrong about prophecy, but he will not miss heaven.

The following, then, are the chief articles of my prophetical creed:

1. I believe that the world will never be completely converted to Christianity by any existing agency, before the end comes. In spite of all that can be done by ministers, churches, schools and missions, the wheat and tares will grow together until the harvest; and when the end comes, it will find the earth in much the same state that it was when the flood came in the days of Noah (Matt. 13:24-30; 24:37-39).

2. I believe that the widespread unbelief, indifference, formalism and wickedness, which are to be seen throughout Christendom, are only what we are taught to expect in God's Word. Troublous times, departures from the faith, evil men waxing worse and worse, love waxing cold, are things distinctly predicted. So far from making me doubt the truth of Christianity, they help to confirm my faith. Melancholy and sorrowful as the sight is, if I did not see it I should think the Bible was not true (Matt. 24:12; 1 Tim. 4:1; 2 Tim. 3: 1, 4, 13).

3. I believe that the grand purpose of the present dispensation is to gather out of the world an elect people, and not to convert all mankind. It does not surprise me at all to hear that the heathen are not all converted when missionaries preach, and that believers are but a little flock in any congregation in my own land. It is precisely the state of things which I expect to find. The gospel is to be preached 'as a witness', and then shall the end come. This is the dispensation of election, and not of universal conversion (Acts 15:14; Matt 24:14).

4. I believe that the second coming of our Lord Jesus Christ is the great event which will wind up the present dispensation, and for which we ought daily to long and pray. 'Thy kingdom come', 'Come, Lord Jesus', should be our daily prayer. We look backward, if we have faith, to Christ dying on the cross, and we ought to look forward no less, if we have hope, to Christ coming again (John 14:3; 2 Tim. 4:8; 2 Peter 3:12).

5. I believe that the second coming of our Lord Jesus Christ will be a real, literal, personal, bodily coming; and that as He went away in the clouds of heaven with His body, before the eyes of men, so in like manner He will return (Acts 1:11).

6. I believe that after our Lord Jesus Christ comes again, the earth shall be renewed, and the curse removed; the devil shall be bound, the godly shall be rewarded, the wicked shall be punished; and that before He comes there shall be neither resurrection, judgment, nor millennium, and that not till after He comes shall the earth be filled with the knowledge of the glory of the Lord (Acts 3:21; Isa. 25:6-0; 1 Thess. 4: 14-18; Rev. 20: 1 etc).

7. I believe that the Jews shall ultimately be gathered again as a separate nation, restored to their own land, and converted to the faith of Christ, after going through great tribulation (Jer. 30:10, 11; 31:10; Rom. 11:25, 26; Dan. 12:1; Zech. 13: 8, 9).

8. I believe that the literal sense of the Old Testament prophecies has been far too much neglected by the Churches, and is far too much neglected at the present day, and that under the mistaken system of *spiritualising and accommodating* Bible language, Christians have too often completely missed its meaning (Luke 24: 25, 26).

9. I do not believe that the preterist scheme of interpreting the Apocalypse, which regards the book as almost entirely *fulfilled* or the futurist scheme, which regards it as almost entirely *unfulfilled*, are either of them to be implicitly followed. The truth, I expect, will be found to lie between the two.

10. I believe that the Roman Catholic Church is the great predicted apostasy from the faith, and is Babylon and antichrist, although I think it highly probably that a more complete development of antichrist will yet be exhibited to the world (2 Thess. 2:3-11; 1 Tim. 4:1-3).

11. Finally, I believe that it is for the safety, happiness and comfort of all true Christians, to expect as little as possible from churches or governments under the present dispensation, to hold themselves ready for tremendous convulsions and changes of all things established, and to expect their good things only from Christ's second advent.

The student of prophecy will see at a glance that there are many subjects on which I abstain from giving an opinion.

About the precise time when the present dispensation will end, about the manner in which the heathen will be converted, about the mode in which the Jews will be restored to their own land, about the burning up of the earth, about the first resurrection, about the rapture of the saints, about the distinction between the appearing and the coming of Christ, about the future siege of Jerusalem and the last tribulation of the Jews, about the binding of Satan before the millennium begins, about the duration of the millennium, about the loosing of Satan at the end of the thousand years, about the destruction of God and Magog, about the precise nature and position of the new Jerusalem, about all these things, I purposely decline expressing my opinion. I could say something about them all, but it would be little better than conjecture. I am thankful that others have more light about them than I have. For myself, I feel unable at present to speak positively. If I have learned anything in studying prophecy, I think I have learned the wisdom of not 'making haste' to decide what is true.

I am well aware that the views I have laid down appear to many persons very gloomy and discouraging. The only answer I make to that charge is this: Are they scriptural? Are they in accordance with the lessons of history and experience? To my mind they certainly are. I see human failure and human corruption stamped on the conclusion of all dispensations preceding our own. I see much in the present state of the world to make me expect that the present dispensation will not end better than those which have gone before. In short, there seems an inherent tendency to decay in everything that man touches. There is no such thing as creature perfection. God is teaching that lesson by all His successive modes of dealing with mankind. There will be no perfection till the Lord comes. The patriarchal, the Mosaic and the Christian dispensations all tend to prove this. Those words of Scripture shall yet be verified, 'I will overturn, it: and it shall be no more, until he come whose right it is; and I will give it Him' (Ezek. 21:27). When the Lord Jesus comes back to earth, and the tabernacle of God is with men, then will there be perfection, but not till then. God will have all the glory at last, and all the world shall confess that without God, man can do nothing. God shall be 'all in all' (1 Cor. 15:28).

The one point on which I desire to fix the eyes of my own soul, is the second personal coming of my Lord and Saviour Jesus Christ. To that 'blessed hope and glorious appearing', I wish, by God's help, to direct all who read this volume. God forbid that anyone should neglect present duties! To sit idly waiting for Christ, and not to attend to the business of our respective positions, is not Christianity, but fanaticism. Let us remember in all our daily employments, that we serve *a Master who is coming again*. If I can only stir up one Christian to think more of that second coming, and to keep it more prominently before his mind, I feel that the volume will not have been published in vain.

If any one ask me why I have chosen this particular period for the republication of these prophetical tracts, I think it is sufficient answer to point to the times in which we live. I do not forget that we are poor judges of our own days, and are very apt to exaggerate their importance. But I doubt much whether there ever was a time in the history of our country, when the horizon on all sides, both political and ecclesiastical, was so thoroughly black and lowering. In every direction we see men's hearts 'failing for fear, and for looking for those things that seem coming on the earth'. Everything around us seems unscrewed, loosened and out of joint. The fountains of the great deep appear to be breaking up. Ancient institutions are tottering, and ready to fall. Social and ecclesiastical systems are failing, and crumbling away. Church and State seem alike convulsed to their very foundations, and what the end of this convulsion may be no man can tell.

Whether the last days of old England have really come, whether her political greatness is about to pass away, whether her Protestant Church is about to have her candlestick removed, whether in the coming crash of nations England is to perish like Amalek, or at length to be saved, and escape 'so as by fire', all these are points which I dare not attempt to settle: a very few years will decide them. But I am sure there never was a time when it was more imperatively needful to summon believers to 'cease from man', to stand on their watchtowers and to build all their hopes on the second coming of the Lord. Happy is he who has learned to expect little from Parliaments or Convocations, from Statesmen or from Bishops, and to look steadily for Christ's appearing! He is the man who will not be disappointed.

1

WATCH

Then shall the kingdom of heaven be likened unto ten virgins, which took their lamps, and went forth to meet the bridegroom. And five of them were wise, and five were foolish. They that were foolish took their lamps, and took no oil with them: But the wise took oil in their vessels with their lamps. While the bridegroom tarried, they all slumbered and slept. And at midnight there was a cry made, Behold, the bridegroom cometh: go ye out to meet him. Then all those virgins arose, and trimmed their lamps. And the foolish said unto the wise, Give us of you oil; for our lamps are gone out. But the wise answered, saying, Not so; lest there be not enough for us and you: but go ye rather to them that sell, and buy for yourselves. And while they went to buy, the bridegroom came; and they that were ready went in with him to the marriage: and the door was shut. Afterward came also the other virgins, saying, Lord, Lord, open to us. But he answered and said, Verily I say unto you, I know you not. Watch therefore, for ye know neither the day nor the hour wherein the Son of man cometh (Matt. 25: 1-13).

The passage of Scripture before our eyes is one that deserves the close attention of all professing Christians. We ought to read it again and again, until we are thoroughly familiar with every sentence that it contains. It is a passage that concerns us all, whether ministers or people, rich or poor, learned or unlearned, old or young. It is a passage that can never be known too well.

These thirteen verses make up one of the most solemn parables that our Lord Jesus Christ ever spoke, partly because of the time at which it was spoken, partly because of the matter which it contains.

As to the *time*, it was but a few days before our Lord's crucifixion. It was spoken within view of Gethsemane and Calvary, of the cross and the grave.

As to the *matter*, it stands as a beacon to the Church of Christ in all ages. It is a witness against carelessness and slothfulness, against apathy and indifference about religion, and a witness of no uncertain sound. It cries to thoughtless sinners, 'Awake!' It cries to true servants of Christ, 'Watch!'

There are many trains of thought which this parable opens up, that I must of necessity leave alone. It would be foreign to my purpose to follow them out. I do not sit down to compose a learned commentary, but to write a simple practical address. I shall only clear my way by explaining two things, which otherwise might not be understood. And when I have done that, I shall keep to those main truths which it is most useful for us to know.

The marriage customs of the country, where the parable was spoken, call for a few words of explanation. Marriages there generally took place in the evening. The bridegroom and his friends came in procession to the bride's house after nightfall. The young women who were the bride's friends were all assembled there, waiting for him. As soon as the lamps and torches, carried by the bridegroom's party, were seen coming in the distance, these young women lighted their lamps, and went forth to meet him. Then, having formed one united party, they all returned together to the bride's home. As soon as they arrived there, they entered in, the doors were shut, the marriage ceremony went forward, and no else was admitted. All these were familiar things to those who heard the Lord Jesus speak; and it is right and proper that you should have them in your mind's eye while you read this parable.

The figures and emblems used in the parable also call for some explanation. I will give you my own view of their meaning. I may be wrong. I freely admit that they are not always interpreted exactly in the same way. But you have a right to have my opinion, and I will give it you shortly and decidedly.

I believe the parable to be a prophecy all the way through.

I believe the time spoken of in the parable, is the time when Christ shall return in person to this world, and a time yet to come. The very first word, the word 'then', compared with the end of the twenty-fourth chapter, appears to me to settle that question.

I believe the ten virgins carrying lamps represent the whole body of professing Christians, the visible Church of Christ.

I believe the bridegroom represents our Lord Jesus Christ Himself.

I take the wise virgins to be the true believers, the real disciples of Christ, the converted part of the visible Church.

I take the foolish to be the mere nominal Christians, the unconverted, the whole company of those who have no vital godliness.[1]

I take the lamps, which all alike carried, to be that mere outward profession of Christianity which every one possesses who has been baptised and has never formally renounced his baptism.

I take the oil, which some virgins had with their lamps, and others had not, to be the grace of the Holy Ghost, that 'unction of the Holy One' which is the mark of all true Christians.

I consider the coming of the bridegroom to mean the second personal coming or advent of the Lord Christ, when He shall return in the clouds with glory.

I consider the going in to the marriage of the wise virgins, to mean the believer's entrance into his full reward in the day of Christ's appearing.

I consider the shutting out of the foolish virgins to mean the exclusion from Christ's kingdom and glory of every soul whom He shall find unconverted at His second advent.

I offer these short explanations to your attention. I am not going to enter into any unprofitable discussion about them. And without saying another word in the way of preface, I will at once go on to point out the great practical lessons which the parable of the ten virgins is meant to teach us.

1. Learn, first of all, that the visible Church of Christ will always be a mixed body till Christ comes again.

2. Learn, secondly, that the visible Church is always in danger of neglecting the doctrine of Christ's second advent.

3. Learn, thirdly, that whenever Christ does come again, it will be a very sudden event.

4. Learn, fourthly, that Christ's second advent will make an immense change to all the members of the visible Church, both good and bad.

Reader, let me try to set each of these four truths plainly before you. If I can bring you, by God's help, to see their vast importance, I believe I shall have done your soul an essential service.

1. Learn, first of all, that *the visible Church of Christ will always be a mixed body, till Christ comes again.*

I can gather no other meaning from the beginning of the parable we are now considering. I see there wise and foolish virgins mingled together in one company, virgins with oil, and virgins with no oil, all side by side. And I see this state of things going on till the very moment the bridegroom appears. I see all this, and I cannot avoid the conclusion that the visible Church will always be a mixed body till Jesus comes again. Its members will never be all unbelievers: Christ will always have His witnesses. Its members will never be all believers: there will always be a vast proportion of formality, unbelief, hypocrisy and false profession.

I frankly say that I can find no standing ground for the common opinion that the visible Church will gradually advance to a state of perfection, that it will become better and better, holier and holier, up to the very end, and that little by little the whole body shall become full of light. I see no warrant of Scripture for believing that sin will gradually dwindle away in the earth, consume, melt and disappear by inches, like the last snowdrift in spring. Nor yet do I see warrant for believing that holiness will gradually increase, like the banyan tree of the East, until it blossoms, blooms and fills the face of the world with fruit. I know that thousands think in this way. All I say is, that I cannot see it in God's Word.

I fully admit that the gospel appears sometimes to make rapid progress in some countries; but that it ever does more than call out an elect people, I utterly deny. It never did more in the days of the Apostles. Out of all the cities that Paul visited, there is not the slightest proof that in any one the whole population became believers. It never has done more in any country, from the time of the Apostle down to the present day. There never yet was a parish or congregation in any part of the world, however favoured in the ministry it enjoyed, there never was one, I believe, in which all the people were converted. At all events, I never read or heard of it, and my belief is the thing never has been, and never will. I believe that now is the time of *election*, not of universal conversion. Now is the time for the *gathering out* of Christ's little flock. The time of general obedience is yet to come.

I fully admit that missions are doing a great work among the heathen, and that schools and district-visiting are rescuing thousands from the devil at home. I do not undervalue these things. I would to God that all professing Christians would value them more. But men appear to me to forget that gospel religion is often withering in one place while it is flourishing in another. They look at the progress of Christianity in the west of Europe. They forget how fearfully it has lost ground in the East. They point to the little floodtide of Tinnevelly and Krishnaghur. They forget the tremendous ebb in North Africa, Egypt and Asia Minor. And as for any signs that all the ends of the earth shall turn to the Lord, under the present order of things, there are none. God's work is going forward, as it always has done. The gospel is being preached for a witness to every quarter of the globe. The elect are being brought to Christ one by one, and there is everything to encourage us to persevere. But more than this, no missionary can report in any station in the world.

I long for the conversion of all mankind as much as anyone. But I believe it is utterly beyond the reach of any instrumentality that man possesses.

I quite expect that the earth will one day be filled with the knowledge of the glory of the Lord. But I believe that day will be an entirely new dispensation: it will not be till after the Lord's return. I would not hesitate to preach the gospel, and offer Christ's salvation to every man and woman alive; but that there always will be a vast amount of unbelief and wickedness until the second advent, I am fully persuaded. The gospel-net may perhaps be spread far more widely than it has been hitherto, but the angels shall find abundance of bad fish in it as well as good, in the last day. The gospel labourers may possibly be multiplied a thousandfold, and I pray God it may be so; but however faithfully they may sow, a large proportion of tares will be found growing together with the wheat, at the time of harvest.

Reader, how is it with your own soul? Remember, that till the Lord Jesus Christ comes again there always will be wise and foolish in the Church. Now, which are you?

The *wise* are they who have that wisdom which the Holy Ghost alone can give. They know their own sinfulness. They know Christ as their own precious Saviour. They know how to walk and please God, and they act upon their knowledge. They look on life as a season of preparation for eternity, not as an end, but as a way, not as a harbour, but as a voyage, not as a home, but as a journey, not as their full age, but their time of school. Happy are they who know these things! The world may despise them, but they are the wise.

The *foolish* are they who are without spiritual knowledge. They neither know God, nor Christ, nor sin, nor their own hearts, nor the world, nor heaven, nor hell, nor the value of their souls as they ought. There is no folly like this. To expect wages after doing no work, or prosperity after taking no pains, or learning after neglecting books, this is rank folly. But to expect heaven without faith in Christ, or the kingdom of God without being born again, or the crown of glory without the cross and a holy walk, all this is greater folly still, and yet more common. Alas! for the folly of the world!

Reader, till the Lord Jesus Christ comes, there always will be some who have grace, and some who have not grace, in the visible Church. Now which are you? How is it with your own soul?

Some have nothing but the name of Christian: others have the reality. Some have only the outward profession of religion: others have the possession also. Some are content if they belong to the Church: others are never content, unless they are also united by faith to Christ. Some are satisfied if they have only the baptism of water: others are never satisfied unless they also feel within the baptism of the Spirit, and the sprinkling of the blood of atonement. Some stop short in the form of Christianity: others never rest until they have also the substance.

Reader, the visible Church of Christ is made up of these two classes. There always have been such. There always will be such until the end. There must, no doubt, be borderers and waverers, whom man's eye cannot make out, though God's eye can. But gracious and graceless, wise and foolish, make up the whole visible Church of Christ.

You yourself are described and written down in this parable. You are either one of the wise virgins, or one of the foolish. You have either got the oil of grace, or you have got none. You are either a member of Christ, or a child of the devil. You are either travelling towards heaven, or towards hell. Never for a moment forget this. This is the point that concerns your soul. Whatever your opinion may be on other points, this is the one that you should never lose sight of. Let not the devil divert your attention from it. Say to yourself, as you read this parable, 'I am spoken of here.'

2. Learn, secondly, that *the visible Church is always in danger of neglecting the doctrine of Christ's second advent.*

I draw this truth from that solemn verse in the parable, 'While the bridegroom tarried, they all slumbered and slept.' I am quite aware that many good men explain these words in a different way. But I dare not call any man master. I feel that I am set for the proclamation of that which my own conscience tells me is true, and I cannot be bound by the opinions of others. There are such things as erroneous interpretations received by tradition, as well as false doctrines received by tradition, and against both I think we ought to be on our guard.

I do not believe that the words, 'they all slumbered and slept', mean the death of all, though many think so. To my mind such an interpretation is contrary to plain facts. All the professing Church will not be sleeping the sleep of death when Jesus comes again. St. Paul himself says in one place, 'We shall not all sleep, but we shall all be changed' (1 Cor. 15:51), and in another, 'We which are alive and remain shall be caught up, to meet the Lord in the air' (1 Thess. 4:17). Now the interpretation of which I speak involves a most awkward contradiction to these two plain texts.

I do not believe that the words were meant to teach us that the whole professing Church will get into a slumbering and sleeping state of soul, though many think so. I would not be misunderstood in saying this. I do not for a moment deny that the love of even the brightest Christians is very cold, and that neither their faith nor works are what they ought to be. All I mean to say is, that this is not the truth which appears to me to be taught here. Such a view of the text seems to me to wipe away that broad line of distinction between believers and unbelievers, which, with all the shortcomings of believers, undoubtedly does exist. Sleep is one of those very emblems which the Spirit has chosen to represent the state of the unconverted man. 'Awake, thou that sleepest,' He says, 'and arise from the dead, and Christ shall give thee light' (Eph. 5:14).

But what does the verse mean? I believe that the words 'all slumbered and slept', are to be interpreted with a special regard to the great event on which the whole parable hinges: even the second advent of Christ. And I believe our Lord's meaning was simply this, that during the interval between His first and second advent, the whole Church, both believers and unbelievers, would get into a dull and dim-sighted state of soul about the blessed doctrine of His own personal return to earth.

And, reader, I say deliberately, that so far as my own judgment goes, there never was a saying of our Lord's more thoroughly verified by the event. I say that of all doctrines of the gospel, the one about which Christians have become most unlike the first Christians, in their sense of its true value, is the doctrine of Christ's second advent. I am obliged to say this of all denominations of Protestants. I know not of any exception. In our view of man's corruption, of justification by faith, of our need of the sanctifying work of the Spirit, of the sufficiency of Scripture, upon these points I believe we should find that English believers were much of one mind with believers at Corinth, Ephesus, Philippi or Rome, in former times. But in our view of the second advent of Christ, I fear we should find there was a mighty difference between us and them, if our experience could be compared. I am afraid we should find that we fall woefully short of them in our estimate of its importance; that in our system of doctrine it is a star of the fifteenth magnitude, while in theirs it was one of the first. In one word, we should discover, that compared to them in this matter, *we slumber and sleep*.

I must speak my mind on this subject, now that I am upon it. I do so most unwillingly. I do so at the risk of giving offence, and of rubbing against the prejudices of many whom I love. But it is a cross I feel it is a duty to take up. And speak I must.

I submit, then, that in the matter of Christ's second coming and kingdom, the Church of Christ has not dealt fairly with the prophecies of the Old Testament. We have gone on far too long refusing to see that there are two personal advents of Christ spoken of in those prophecies, an advent in humiliation, and an advent in glory, an advent to suffer, and an advent to reign, a personal advent to carry the cross and a personal advent to wear the crown. We have been 'slow of heart to believe *all* that the Prophets have written' (Luke 24:25). The Apostles went into one extreme: they stumbled at Christ's sufferings. We have gone into the other extreme: we have stumbled at Christ's glory. We have got into a confused habit of speaking of the kingdom of Christ as already set up amongst us, and have shut our eyes to the fact that the devil is still prince of this world, and served by the vast majority; and that our Lord, like David in Adullam, though annointed, is not yet set upon His throne. We have got into a vicious habit of taking all the promises spiritually, and all the denunciations and threats literally. The denunciations against Babylon and Nineveh, and Edom, and Tyre, and Egypt, and the rebellious Jews, we have been content to take *literally* and hand over to our neighbours. The blessings and promises of glory to Zion, Jerusalem, Jacob and Israel, we have taken *spiritually*, and comfortably applied them to ourselves and the Church of Christ. To bring forward proofs of this would be a waste of time. No man can hear many sermons, and read many commentaries, without being aware that it is a fact.

Now I believe this to have been an unfair system of interpreting Scripture. I hold that the first and primary sense of every Old Testament promise as well as threat is the *literal* one, and that Jacob means Jacob, Jerusalem means Jerusalem, Zion means Zion, and Israel means Israel, as much as Egypt means Egypt, and Babylon means Babylon. That primary sense, I believe, we have sadly lost sight of. We have adapted and accommodated to the Church of Christ the promises that were spoken by God to Israel and Zion. I do not mean to say that this accommodation is in no sense allowable. But I do mean to say that the primary sense of every prophecy and promise in the Old Testament prophecy was intended to have a literal fulfilment, and that this literal fulfilment has been far too much put aside and thrust into a corner. And by so doing I think we have exactly fulfilled our Lord's words in the parable of the ten virgins, we have proved that we are *slumbering and sleeping* about the second advent of Christ.

But I submit further, that in the interpretation of the New Testament, the Church of Christ has dealt almost as unfairly with our Lord's second advent, as she has done in the interpretation of the Old. Men have got into the habit of putting a strange sense upon many of those passages which speak of 'the coming of the Son of Man', or of the Lord's 'appearing'. And this habit has been far too readily submitted to. Some tell us that the coming of the Son of Man often means death. No one can read the thousands of epitaphs in churchyards, in which some text about the coming of Christ is thrust in, and not perceive how widespread this view is. Some tell us that our Lord's coming means the destruction of Jerusalem. This is a very common way of interpreting the expression. Many find the literal Jerusalem everywhere in New Testament prophecies, though, oddly enough, they refuse to see it in Old Testament prophecies, and, like Aaron's rod, they make it swallow up everything else. Some tell us that our Lord's coming means the general judgment, and the end of all things. This is their one answer to all inquiries about things to come.

Now I believe that all these interpretations are entirely beside the mark. I have not the least desire to underrate the importance of such subjects as death and judgment. I willingly concede that the destruction of Jerusalem is typical of many things connected with our Lord's second advent, and is spoken of in chapters where that mighty event is foretold. But I must express my own firm belief that the coming of Christ is one distinct thing, and that death, judgment and the destruction of Jerusalem, are three other distinct things.

And the wide acceptance which these strange interpretations have met with I hold to be one more proof that in the matter of Christ's second advent the Church has long *slumbered and slept*.

The plain truth of Scripture I believe to be as follows. When the number of the elect is accomplished, Christ will come again to this world with power and great glory. He will raise His saints, and gather them to Himself. He will punish with fearful judgments all who are found His enemies, and reward with glorious rewards all His believing people. He will take to Himself His great power and reign, and establish an universal kingdom. He will gather the scattered tribes of Israel and place them once more in their own land. As He came the first time in person, so He will come the second time in person. As He went away from earth visibly, so He will return visibly. As He literally rode upon an ass, was literally sold for thirty pieces of silver, had His hands and feet literally pierced, was numbered literally with the transgressors and had lots literally cast upon His raiment, and all that Scripture might be fulfilled so also will He literally come, literally set up a kingdom and literally reign over the earth, because the very same Scripture has said it shall be so.

The words of the angels, in the first of Acts, are plain and unmistakable: This same Jesus which is taken up from you into heaven, shall so come in like manner as ye have seen Him go into heaven. (Acts 1:11).

So also the words of the Apostle Peter:

The times of refreshing shall come from the presence of the Lord; and He shall send Jesus Christ, which before was preached unto you: whom the heavens must receive until the times of restitution of all things, which God hath spoken by the mouth of all His holy prophets since the world began (Acts 3:19-21).

So also the words of the Psalmist:

When the Lord shall build up Zion He shall appear in His glory (Ps. 102:16).

So also the words of Zechariah:

The Lord my God shall come, and all the saints with thee (Zech. 14:5).

So also the words of Isaiah:

The Lord of hosts shall reign in Mount Zion, and in Jerusalem, and before His ancients gloriously (Isa. 24:23).

So also the words of Jeremiah:

I will bring again the captivity of my people Israel and Judah, saith the Lord, and I will cause them to return to the land that I gave to their fathers, and they shall possess it. I will bring again the captivity of Jacob's tents, and have mercy on his dwelling-place; and the city shall be built on her own heap (Jer. 30: 3, 18).

So also the words of Daniel:

Behold one like the Son of Man came with the clouds of heaven, and came to the Ancient of Days, and they brought Him near before Him. And there was given Him dominion, and glory, and a kingdom, that all people, nations, and languages should serve Him; His dominion is an everlasting dominion, which shall not pass away; and His kingdom that which shall not be destroyed (Dan. 7: 13, 14).

All these texts are to my mind plain prophecies of Christ's second coming and kingdom. All are yet without their accomplishment, and all shall yet be literally and exactly fulfilled.

I say 'literally and exactly fulfilled' and I say so advisedly. From the first day that I began to read the Bible with my heart, I have never been able to see these texts, and hundreds like them, in any other light. It always seemed to me that as we take literally the texts foretelling that the walls of Bablyon shall be cast down, so we ought to take literally the texts foretelling that the walls of Zion shall be built up, that as according to prophecy the Jews were literally scattered, so according to prophecy the Jews will be literally gathered, and that as the least and minutest predictions were made good on the subject of our Lord's coming to suffer, so the minutest predictions shall be made good which describe our Lord's coming to reign. And I have long felt it is one of the greatest shortcomings of the Church of Christ that we ministers do not preach enough about this advent of Christ, and that private believers do not think enough about it. A few of us here and there received the doctrine, and profess to love it; but the number of such persons is comparatively very small. And, after all, none of us live on it, feed on it, act on it, work from it, take comfort in it, as much as God intended us to do. In short, the Bridegroom tarries, and we all *slumber and sleep*.

It proves nothing against the doctrine of Christ's second coming and kingdom, that it has sometimes been fearfully abused. I should like to know what doctrine of the gospel has not been abused. Salvation by grace has been made a pretext for licentiousness, election, an excuse for all manner of unclean living and justification by faith, a warrant for Antinomianism. But if men will draw wrong conclusions we are not therefore obliged to throw aside good principles. We do not give up the gospel because of the outrageous conduct of the Anabaptists of Munster, or the extravagant assertions of Saltmarsh and William Huntingdon, or the strange proceedings of Jumpers and Shakers. And where is the fairness of telling us that we ought to reject the second advent of Christ because there were Fifth Monarchy Men in the days of the Commonwealth, and Irvingites and Millerites in our own time. Alas, men must be hard pressed for an argument when they have no better reasons than this!

It proves nothing against the second advent of Christ, that those who hold the doctrine differ among themselves on many particular points in prophecy. Such differences need never stumble any one who recollects that unity on great points is perfectly consistent with disagreement on small ones.

23

Luther and Zwingli differed widely in their views of the Lord's Supper: yet who would think of saying that therefore Protestantism is all false? Fletcher and Toplady were both clergymen in the Church of England, but differed widely about Calvinism: yet where would be the sense of saying that all Evangelical religion was therefore untrue? In common fairness this ought to be remembered when people talk of the differences among those who study prophecy. It is possible for men to differ much as to the meaning they place on the symbols in the book of Revelation, and yet on the matter of Christ's coming and kingdom they may be entirely and substantially agreed.

It proves nothing against the doctrine that it is encompassed with many difficulties. This I fully concede. The order of events connected with our Lord's coming, and the manner of His kingdom when it is set up, are both deep subjects, and hard to be understood. But I firmly believe that the difficulties connected with any other system of interpreting unfulfilled prophecy, are just twice as many as those which are said to stand in our way. I believe too that the difficulties connected with our Lord's second coming are not half so many as those connected with His first, and that it was a far more improbable thing, 'a priori' that the Son of God should come to *suffer*, than it is that He should come to *reign*. And, after all, what have we to do with the 'how' and 'in what manner' prophecies are to be fulfilled? Is our miserable understanding of what is possible to be the measure and limit of God's dealings? The only question we have to do with is, 'Has God said a thing?' If He has, we ought not to doubt it shall be done.

For myself, I can only give my own individual testimony; but the little I know experimentally of the doctrine of Christ's second coming, makes me regard it as most practical and precious and makes me long to see it more generally received.

I find it a powerful spring and stimulus to holy living, a motive for patience, for moderation, for spiritual-mindedness, a test for the employment of time and a gauge for all my actions: 'Should I like my Lord to find me in this place, should I like him to find me so doing?'

I find it the strongest argument for missionary work. The time is short. The Lord is at hand. The gathering out from all nations will soon be accomplished, the heralds and forerunners of the King will soon have proclaimed the gospel in every nation. The night is far spent. The King will soon be here.

I find it the best answer to the infidel. He sneers at our churches and chapels, at our sermons and services, at our tracts and our schools. He points to the millions who care nothing for Christianity, after 1,800 years of preaching. He asks me how I can account for it, if Christianity be true? I answer, it was never said that all the world would believe, and serve Christ under the present dispensation. I tell him the state of things he ridicules was actually foreseen, and the number of true Christians, it was predicted, would be few. But I tell him that Christ's kingdom is yet to come; and that though we see not yet all things put under Him, they will be so one day.

I find it the best argument with the Jew. If I do not take all the prophecy of Isaiah literally, I know not how I can persuade him that the fifty-third chapter is literally fulfilled. But if I do, I have a resting place for my lever, which I know he cannot shake. How men can expect the Jews to see a Messiah coming to suffer in Old Testament prophecies, if they do not themselves see in them a Messiah coming to reign, is past my understanding.

And now, is there any one among the readers of this address who cannot receive the doctrine of Christ's second advent and kingdom? I invite him to consider the subject calmly and dispassionately. Dismiss from your mind traditional interpretations. Separate the doctrine from the mistakes and blunders of many who hold it. Do not reject the foundation because of the wood, hay and stubble which some have built upon it. Do not condemn it and cast it aside because of injudicious friends. Only examine the texts which speak of it, as calmly and fairly as you weigh texts in the Romish, Arian or Socinian controversies, and I am hopeful as to the result on your mind. Alas, if texts of Scripture were always treated by those who dislike the doctrine of Christ's second advent, I should indeed tremble for the cause of truth!

Is there any one among the readers of this address who agrees with the principles I have tried to advocate? I beseech that man to endeavour to realise the second coming of Christ more and more. Truly we feel it but little compared to what we ought to do, at the very best. Be gentle in argument with those that differ from you. Remember that a man may be mistaken on this subject, and yet be a holy child of God. It is not the slumbering on this subject that ruins souls, but the want of grace!

Above all, avoid dogmatism and positiveness, and specially about symbolical prophecy. It is a sad truth, but a truth never to be forgotten, that none have injured the doctrine of the second coming so much as its over-zealous friends.

3. Learn, in the third place, that *whenever Christ does come again, it will be a very sudden event.*

I draw that truth from the verse in the parable which says, 'At midnight there was a cry made, Behold, the bridegroom cometh, go ye out to meet him.'

I do not know when Christ will come again. I should think it most presumptuous if I said that I did. I am no prophet, though I love the subject of prophecy. I dislike all fixing of dates, and naming of years, and I believe it has done great harm. I only assert positively that Christ will come again one day to set up His kingdom on earth, and that whether the day be near or whether it be far off, it will take the Church and the world exceedingly by surprise.

It will come on men suddenly. It will break on the world all at once. It will not have been talked over, prepared for and looked forward to by everybody. It will awaken men's minds like the cry of fire at midnight. It will startle men's hearts like a trumpet blown at their bedside in their first sleep. Like Pharaoh and his host in the Red Sea, they will know nothing till the very waters are upon them. Like Dathan, and Abiram, and their company, when the earth opened under them, the moment of their hearing the report of the visitation will be the same moment when they will see it with their eyes. Before they can recover their breath and know where they are, they shall find that the Lord is come.

I suspect there is a vague notion floating in men's minds that the present order of things will not end quite so suddenly. I suspect men cling to the idea that there will be a kind of Saturday night in the world, a time when all will know the day of the Lord is near; a time when all will be able to cleanse their consciences, look at their wedding garments, shake off their earthly business and prepare to meet their God. If any reader of this address has got such a notion into his head, I charge him to give it up for ever.

If anything is clear in unfulfilled prophecy, this one fact seems clear, that the Lord's coming will be sudden, and take men by surprise. And any view of prophecy which destroys the possibility of its being sudden – whether by interposing a vast number of events as yet to happen, or by placing the millenium between ourselves and the advent – any such view appears to my mind to carry with it a fatal defect. Everything which is written in Scripture on this point confirms the truth, that Christ's second coming will be sudden. 'As a snare shall it come', says one place, 'As a thief in the night,' says another. 'As the lightning', says a third, 'In such an hour as ye think not,' says a fourth. 'When they shall say, Peace and safety,' says a fifth (Luke 21:35; 1 Thess. 5:2; Luke 17:24; Matt. 24: 44; 1 Thess. 5:3).

Our Lord Jesus Christ Himself uses two most striking comparisons, when dwelling on this subject. Both are most teaching, and both ought to raise in us solemn thoughts. In one He compares His coming to the days of Lot. In the days when Lot fled from Sodom, the men of Sodom were buying and selling, eating and drinking, planting and building. They thought of nothing but earthly things: they were entirely absorbed in them. They despised Lot's warning. They mocked at his counsel. The sun rose on the earth as usual. All things were going on as they had done for hundreds of years. They saw no sign of danger. But now mark what our Lord says: 'The same day that Lot went out of Sodom, it rained fire and brimstone from heaven, and destroyed them all. Even thus shall it be in the day when the Son of Man is revealed' (Luke 17:28-30).

In the other passage I allude to, our Lord compares His coming to the days of Noah. Do you remember how it was in Noah's day? Stay a little, and let me remind you. When the flood came on the earth in Noah's time, there was no appearance beforehand of anything so awful being near. The days and nights were following each other in regular succession. The grass and trees and crops were growing as usual. The business of the world was going on. And though Noah preached continually of coming danger, and warned men to repent, no one believed what he said. But at last, one day the rain began and did not cease: the waters rose and did not stop; the flood came, and swelled, and went on, and covered one thing after another; and all were drowned who were not in the ark. Now mark what our Lord says: 'As it was in the days of Noah, so shall it also be in the days of the Son of Man: they did eat, they drank, they married wives, they were given in marriage, until the day that Noah entered into the ark, and the flood came and destroyed them all' (Luke 17: 26, 27). The flood took the world by surprise, so also will the coming of the Son of Man. In the midst of the world's business, when everything is going on just as usual, in such an hour as this the Lord Jesus Christ will return.

Reader, the suddenness of the Lord's second advent is a truth that should lead every professing Christian to great searchings of heart. It should lead him to serious thought, both about himself and about the world.

Think for a moment how little the world is prepared for such an event. Look at the towns and cities of the earth, and think of them. Mark how most men are entirely absorbed in the things of time, and utterly engrossed with the business of their callings. Banks, counting-houses, shops, politics, law, medicine, commerce, railways, banquets, balls, theatres, each and all are drinking up the hearts and souls of thousands, and thrusting out the things of God. Think what a fearful shock the sudden stoppage of all these things would be, the sudden stoppage which will be in the day of Christ's appearing. If only one great house of business stops payment now, it makes a great sensation. What then shall be the crash when the whole machine of worldly affairs shall stand still at once? From money counting and earthly scheming, from racing after riches and wrangling about trifles, to be hurried away to meet the King of kings, how tremendous the change! From dancing and dressing, from opera going and novel reading to be summoned away by the voice of the archangel and the trump of God, how awful the transition! Yet remember, all this shall one day be.

Look at the rural parishes of such a land as ours, and think of them. See how the minds of the vast majority of their inhabitants are buried in farms and allotments, in cattle and corn, in rent and wages, in rates and tithes, in digging and sowing, in buying and selling, in planting and building. See how many there are who evidently care for nothing, and feel nothing, excepting the things of this world; who reckoned nothing whether their minister preaches law or gospel, Christ or antichrist, and would be utterly unconcerned if the Archbishop of Canterbury was turned out of Lambeth Palace, and the Pope of Rome put in his place. See how many there are of whom it can only be said that their bellies and their pockets are their gods. And then fancy the awful effect of a sudden call to meet the Lord Christ, a call to a day of reckoning, in which the price of wheat and the rate of wages shall be nothing, and the Bible shall be the only rule of trial! And yet remember, all this shall one day be.

Reader, picture these things to your mind's eye. Picture your own house, your own family, your own fireside. What will be found there? Picture, above all, your own feelings, your own state of mind. And then, remember, that this is the end towards which the world is hastening. There will be no long notice to quit. This is the way in which the world's affairs will be wound up. This is an event which may possibly happen in your own time. And surely you cannot avoid the conclusion that the second coming of Christ is no mere curious speculation. It is an event of vast practical importance to your own soul.

'Ah!' I can imagine some reader saying, 'This is all foolishness, raving, and nonsense; this writer is beside himself. This is all extravagant fanaticism. Where is the likelihood, where is the probability of all this? The world is going on as it always did. The world will last my time.' Do not say so. Do not drive away the subject by such language as this. This is the way that men talked in the days of Noah and Lot, but what happened? They found to their cost that Noah and Lot were right. Do not say so. The Apostle Peter foretold, eighteen hundred years ago, that men would talk in this way. 'There shall come in the last day scoffers,' he tells us, 'saying, Where is the promise of His coming? for since the fathers fell asleep, all things continue as they were from the beginning of the creation' (2 Peter 3:3, 4). Oh, do not fulfil his prophecy by your unbelief!

Where is the raving fanaticism of the things which I have been saying? Show it to me if you can. I calmly assert that the present order of things will come to an end one day. Will any one deny that? Will any one tell me we are to go on as we do now for ever? I calmly say that Christ's second coming will be the end of the present order of things. I have said so because the Bible says it. I have calmly said that Christ's second coming will be a sudden event, whenever it may be, and may possibly be in our own time. I have said so, because thus and thus I find it written in the Word of God. If you do not like it, I am sorry for it. One thing only you must remember, you are finding fault with the Bible, not with me.

4. Learn, in the last place, that *Christ's second coming will make an immense change to all members of the visible Church, both good and bad.*

I draw this truth from the concluding portion of the parable: from the discovery of the foolish virgins that their lamps were gone out; from their anxious address to the wise, 'Give us of your oil'; from their vain knocking at the door when too late, crying, 'Lord, Lord, open to us'; from the happy admission of the wise who were found ready, in company with the bridegroom. Each and all of these points are full of food for thought. But I have neither time nor space to dwell upon them particularly. I can only take one single broad view of all. To all who have been baptised in the name of Christ, converted or unconverted, believers or unbelievers, holy or unholy, godly or ungodly, wise or foolish, gracious or graceless, to all the second advent of Christ will be an immense change.

It will be an *immense change to the ungodly,* to all who are found mere nominal Christians, a change both in their opinions and position.

All such persons, when Christ comes again, will see the value of real spiritual religion, if they never saw it before. They will do in effect what the parable describes under a figure, they will cry to the godly, 'Give us of your oil, for our lamps are gone out.'

Who does not know, that, as things are now, spiritual religion never brings a man the world's praise? It never has done, and it never does at this day. It entails on a man the world's disapprobation, the world's persecution, the world's mockery, the world's opposition, the world's ridicule, the world's sneers. The world will let a man serve the devil and go to hell quietly, and no one lifts a little finger to stop him, or says, 'Be merciful to your soul.' The world will never let a man serve Christ and go to heaven quietly; everybody cries, 'Hold hard', and does everything that can be done to keep him back.

Who has not heard of nicknames in plenty, bestowed on those who follow Christ, and try to be saved – Pietists, Puritans, Methodists, Fanatics, Enthusiasts, Calvinists, Ultra-religionists, the Saints, the Righteous overmuch, the Very Good People and many more? Who does not know the petty family persecutions which often go on in private society in our day? Let a young person go to every ball, and opera, and racecourse, and worldly party, and utterly neglect his soul, and no one interferes; no one says, 'Spare thyself', no one says, 'Take care: remember God, judgment and eternity.' But let him only begin to read his Bible and be diligent in prayer, let him decline worldly amusements and become particular in his employment of time, let him seek an evangelical ministry and live like an immortal being; let him do this, I say, and all his friends and relations will probably be up in arms. 'You are going too far. You need not be so very good. You are taking up extreme views.' This, in all probability, is the very least that such a person will hear. If a young woman, she will be marked and avoided by all her equals. If a young man, he will be set down by all who know him, as weak, silly and precise. In short, such a person will soon discover that there is no help from the world in the way to heaven, but plenty of help in the way to hell.

Alas, that it should be so: but so it is! These are ancient things. As it was in the days of Cain and Abel, as it was in the days of Isaac and Ishmael, even so it is now. 'They that are born after the flesh will persecute those that are born after the Spirit' (Gal. 4:29). The cross of Christ will always bring reproach with it. As the Jews hated Christ, so the world hates Christians. As the Head was bruised, so also the members will be. As contempt was poured on the Master, so it will be also on the disciples. In short, if a man will become a decided evangelical Christian, in the present order of things, he must 'count the cost' and make up his mind to lose the world's favour. In a word, he must be content to be thought by many little better than a fool.

Reader, there will be an end of all this when Christ returns to this world. The light of that day will at length show everything in its true colours. The scales will fall from the poor worldling's eyes. The value of the soul will flash on his astonished mind. The utter uselessness of a mere nominal Christianity will burst upon him like a thunderstorm. The blessedness of regeneration and faith in Christ, and a holy walk, will shine before him like 'Mene, Mene, Tekel, Peres' on the wall of the Babylonian palace. The veil will fall from his face. He will discover that the godly have been the wise, and that he has played the fool exceedingly. And just as Saul wanted Samuel when it was too late, and Belshazzar sent for Daniel when the kingdom was about to be taken from him, so will the ungodly turn to the very men they once mocked and despised, and cry to them, 'Give us your oil, for our lamps are gone out.'

But as there will be a complete change in the *feelings* of the ungodly, in the day *of* Christ's second advent, so will there also be a complete change in their *position*. Hope, the plank to which they now cling, and on which they generally depend to the very last, hope will be entirely taken away in that awful day. They will seek salvation with earnestness, but not be able to find it. They will run hither and thither in a vain search for the oil of grace. They will knock loudly at the door of mercy, and get no answer. They will cry, 'Lord, Lord, open to us' but all to no purpose. They will discover to their sorrow that opportunities once let slip can never be regained, and that the notion of universal mercy always to be obtained, is a mere delusion of the devil.

Who does not know that thousands are urged to pray and repent now, who never attempt it? They mean to try one day perhaps. Like Felix, they hope for a convenient season. They fancy it will never be too late to seek the Lord. But there is a time coming when prayer shall be heard no longer, and repentance shall be unavailing. There is a time when the door by which Manasseh and Saul the persecutor entered, shall be shut and opened no more. There is a time when the fountain, in which Magdalene, and John Newton, and thousands of others were washed and made clean, shall be sealed for ever. There is a time: when men shall know the folly of sin, but like Judas too late for repentance; when they shall desire to enter the promised land, but like Israel at Kadesh not be able; when they shall see the value of God's favour and covenant blessing, but like Esau when they can longer possess it; when they shall believe every jot and tittle of God's revealed Word, but like the miserable devils only to tremble.

Yes, reader, men may come to this, and many will come to this in the day of Christ's appearing. They will ask and not receive! They will seek and not find. They will knock and the door shall not be opened to them. Alas,

31

indeed, that so it should be. Woe to the man who puts off seeking his manna till the Lord's day of return! Like Israel of old, he will find none. Woe to the man who goes to buy oil when he ought to be burning it! Like the foolish virgins, he will find himself shut out from the marriage supper of the Lamb. Oh, that professing Christians would consider these things! Oh, that they would remember the words of our Lord have yet to be fulfilled:

> When once the Master of the house is risen up, and hath shut to the door, and ye begin to stand without, and to knock at the door, saying, Lord, Lord, open unto us; and He shall answer and say unto you, I know you not whence ye are: then shall ye begin to say, We have eaten and drunk in Thy presence, and Thou hast taught in our streets. But He shall say, I tell you, I know you not whence ye are; depart from Me, all ye workers of iniquity (Luke 13:25-27).

But as Christ's second coming will be a mighty change to the ungodly, so will it also be a *mighty change to the godly*.

They shall at length be freed from everything which now mars their comfort. 'The door shall be shut: Against the fiery darts of Satan, against the loathsome weakness of the flesh which now clings to them, against the unkind world which now misrepresents and misunderstands them, against the doubts and fears which now so often darken their path, against the weariness which now clogs their best efforts to serve the Lord, against coldness and deadness, against shortcomings and backslidings, against all these the door shall be shut for ever. Not one single Canaanite shall be found in the land. They shall no longer be vexed by temptation, persecuted by the world, warred against by the devil. Their conflict shall all be over. Their strife with the flesh shall for ever cease. The armour of God, which they have so long worn, shall at length be laid aside. They shall be where there is no Satan, no sorrow, and no sin.' Ah, reader, the second Eden shall be far better than the first. In the first Eden the door was not shut; our joy was but for a moment. But, blessed be God, in the second Eden, the Lord shall 'shut us in'.

And as the godly shall enjoy freedom from all evil in the day of Christ's appearing, so shall they also enjoy the presence of all good. They shall go in with the Bridegroom to the marriage. They shall be for ever in the company of Christ, and go out no more. Faith shall then be swallowed up in sight. Hope shall become certainty. Knowledge shall at length be perfect. Prayer shall be turned into praise. Desires shall receive their full accomplishment. Hunger and thirst after conformity to Christ's image shall at length be satisfied. The thought of parting shall not spoil the pleasure of meeting. The company of saints shall be enjoyed without hurry and distraction. The family of Abraham shall no more feel temptations; nor the family of Job, afflictions; nor the family of David, household bereavements; nor the family of Paul, thorns in the flesh; nor the family of Lazarus, poverty and sores. Every tear shall be wiped away in that day. It is the time when the Lord shall say, 'I make all things new.'

Oh, reader, if God's children find joy and peace in believing even now, what tongue shall tell their feelings when they behold the King in His beauty! If the report of the land that is far off has been sweet to them in the wilderness, what pen shall describe their happiness, when they see it with their own eyes? If it has cheered them now and then to meet two or three like-minded in this evil world, how their hearts will burn within them when they see a multitude that no man can number, the least defects of each purged away, and not one false brother in the list! If the narrow way has been a way of pleasantness to the scattered few who travelled it with their poor frail bodies, how precious shall their rest seem in the day of gathering together, when they shall have a glorious body like their Lord's! Then shall we understand the meaning of the text, 'In Thy presence is fulness of joy, and at Thy right hand are pleasures evermore' (Psalm 16:11). Then shall we experience the truth of that beautiful hymn, which says:

Let me be with Thee where Thou art,
My Saviour, my eternal rest;
Then only shall this longing heart
Be fully and for ever blest.

Let me be with Thee where Thou art,
Thy unveil'd glory to behold;
Then only shall this wand'ring heart
Cease to be false to Thee, and cold.

Let me be with Thee where Thou art,
Where none can die, where none remove;
There neither death nor life shall part
Me from Thy presence and Thy love.

Is there a man or woman among the readers of this address who ever laughs at true religion? Is there one who persecutes and ridicules vital godliness in others, and dares to talk of people being over-particular, and righteous overmuch? Oh, beware what you are doing! Again I say, beware! You may live to think very differently. You may live to alter your opinion, but perhaps too late. Ah, reader, there is a day before us all when there will be no infidels! No: not one! There is a day when the disciples of Paine, and Voltaire, and Emerson, shall call on the rocks to fall on them, and on the hills to cover them. Before the throne of Jesus every knee shall bow, and every tongue confess that He is the Lord. Remember that day, and beware.

Is there among the readers of this address some dear child of God, who is mocked and despised for the gospel's sake, and feels as if he stood alone? Take comfort. Be patient. 'Wait a little longer.' Your turn shall yet come. When the spies returned from searching Canaan, men talked of stoning Caleb and Joshua, because they brought a good report of the land. A few days passed away, and all the assembly confessed that they alone had been right. Strive to be like them. Follow the Lord, fully, as they did, and sooner or later all men shall confess that you did well. Never, never be afraid of going too far. Never, never be afraid of being too holy. Never, never be ashamed of desiring to go to heaven, and of seeking to have a great crown. Millions will lament in the day of Christ's return, because they have not got religion enough: not one will be heard to say that he has got too much. Take comfort. Press on.

And now, reader, it only remains for me to close this paper by three words of application, which seem to me to arise naturally out of the parable of which I have been writing. I heartily pray God to bless them to your soul, and to make them words in season.

1. My first word of application shall be *a question*. I take the parable of the ten virgins as my warrant, and I address that question to every one of my readers. I ask you, 'Are you ready?' Remember the words of the Lord Jesus, 'They that were ready went in with the bridegroom to the marriage': they that were ready and none else. Now here, in the sight of God, I ask each and every reader, is this your case? Are you ready?

I do not ask whether you are a churchman, and make a profession of religion. I do not ask whether you attend an evangelical ministry, and like evangelical people, and can talk of evangelical subjects, and read evangelical tracts and bookseller, and may be easily attained. I want to search your heart more thoroughly, and probe your conscience more deeply. I want to know whether you have been born again, and whether you have got the Holy Ghost dwelling in your soul. I want to know whether you have any oil in your vessel while you carry the lamp of profession, and whether you are ready to meet the Bridegroom, ready for Christ's return to the earth. I want to know, if the Lord should come this week, whether you could lift up your head with joy, and say, 'This is our God; we have waited for Him; let us be glad, and rejoice in His salvation.' These things I want to know, and this is what I mean when I say, 'Are you ready?'

"Ah!' I can imagine some saying, 'this is asking far too much. *To be ready for Christ's appearing!* this is far too high a standard. This is extravagance. There would be no living in the world at this rate. This is a hard saying. Who can hear it?' I cannot help it. I believe this is the standard of the Bible. I believe this is the standard Paul sets before us when he says the Thessalonians were 'waiting for the Son of God from heaven', and the Corinthians 'waiting for the coming of our Lord Jesus Christ' (1 Thess. 1:10; 1 Cor. 1:7). And surely this is the standard Peter sets before us, when he speaks of 'looking for and hasting unto the coming of the day of God' (2 Peter 3:12). I believe it is a mark that every true believer should be continually aiming at, to live so as to be ever ready to meet Christ. God forbid that I should place the standard of Christian practice a hair's breadth higher than the level at which the Bible places it. But God forbid that I should ever put it a hair's breadth lower. If I do, what right have I to say that the Bible is my rule of faith?

I want to disqualify no man for usefulness upon earth. I require no man to become a hermit, and cease to serve his generation. I call on no man to leave his lawful calling, and neglect his earthly affairs. But I do call on every one to live like one who expects Christ to return: to live soberly, righteously and godly in this present world; to live like a pilgrim and a stranger, ever looking unto Jesus; to live like a good pilgrim and a stranger, ever looking unto Jesus; to live like a good servant, with his loins girded, and his lamp burning; to live like one whose treasure is in heaven, with his heart packed up and ready to be gone. This is readiness. This is preparation. And is this too much to ask? I say unhesitatingly that it is not.

Now, reader, are you ready in this way? If not, I should like to know what good your religion does you. What is it all but a burdensome form? What is it but a mere temporary cloak that will not wear beyond this world? Truly a religion that does not make a man ready for every thing, for death, for judgment, for the second advent, for the resurrection, such a religion may well be looked on with suspicion. Reader, if your religion does not make you ready for anything, you may depend, the sooner it is changed the better.

2. My second word of application shall be an *invitation*. I address it to everyone who feels in his conscience that he has no grace in his heart, to everyone who feels that the character of the foolish virgins is his own. To every such person I give an invitation this day, in my Master's name. I invite you 'to awake and flee to Christ'.

Reader, if you are a man of this sort, you know that all within you is wrong in the sight of God. Nothing can be said more true about you than that you are asleep, asleep not merely about the doctrine of Christ's second advent, but about everything that concerns your soul. You are wide awake perhaps about temporal things. You read the newspapers, it may be, and are mighty in the 'Times'. You have your head stored with earthly wisdom and useful knowledge. But you have no heartfelt sense of sin, no peace or friendship with God, no experimental acquaintance with Christ, no delight in the Bible and prayer. And yet you are a sinner, a dying sinner, an immortal sinner, a sinner going to meet Christ, a sinner going to be judged, What, I would put it to your conscience as an honest man, what is all this but being asleep?

How long is this to go on? When do you mean to arise and live as if you had a soul? when will you cease to hear as one who hears not? When will you give up running after shadows, and seek something substantial? When will you throw off the mockery of a religion which cannot satisfy, cannot comfort, cannot sanctify, cannot save and will not bear a calm examination? When will you give up having a faith which does not influence your practice, having a book which you say is God's Word, but treat as if it was not, having the name of Christian, but knowing nothing of Christ? Oh! reader, when, when shall it once be?

Why not this very year? Why not this very day? Why not at once awake and call upon your God, and resolve that you will sleep no longer? I set before you an open door. I set before you Jesus Christ the Saviour, who died to make atonement for sinners, Jesus who is able to save to the uttermost, Jesus willing to receive. The hand that was nailed to the cross is held out to you in mercy. The eye that wept over Jerusalem is looking on you with pity. The voice that has said to many wanderers, 'Thy sins are forgiven', is saying to you, 'Come to Me.' Go to Jesus first and foremost, if you would know what step to take. Think not to wait for repentance, and faith, and a new heart, but go to Him just as you are. God to Him in prayer, and cry, 'Lord save me, or I perish. I am weary of sleeping; I would fain sleep no longer.' Oh! awake, thou that sleepest, and Christ shall give thee light.

Sun, moon and stars are all witnessing against you: they continue in accordance to God's ordinances, and you are ever transgressing them. The grass, the birds, the very worms of the earth are all witnessing against you: they fill their place in creation, and you do not. Sabbaths and ordinances are continually witnessing against you: they are ever proclaiming that there is a God and a judgment, and you are living as if there were none. The tears and prayers of godly relations are witnessing against you: others are sorrowfully thinking you have a soul, though you seem to forget it. The very gravestones that you see every week are witnessing against you: they are silently witnessing that life is uncertain, time is short, the resurrection is yet to come, the Lord is at hand. All, all are saying, Awake, awake, awake! Oh! reader, the time past may surely suffice you to have slept. Awake to be wise. Awake to be safe. Awake to be happy. Awake, and sleep no more.

3. My last word of application shall be *an exhortation* to all true believers, to all who have the oil of grace in their hearts, and have fled for pardon to the blood of the Lamb. I draw it from the words of the Lord Jesus at the end of the parable. I exhort you earnestly 'to watch'.

I exhort you to watch against everything which might interfere with a readiness for Christ's appearing. Search your own hearts. Find out the things which most frequently interrupt your communion with Christ, and cause fogs to rise between you and the sun. Mark these things, and know them, and against them ever watch and be on your guard.

Watch against sin of every kind and description. Think not to say of any sin whatever, Ah! that is one of the things that I shall never do.' I tell you there is no possible sin too abominable for the very best of us all to commit. Remember David and Uriah. The spirit may be sometimes very willing, but the flesh is always very weak. You are yet in the body. Watch and pray.

Watch against the doubts and unbelief as to the complete acceptance of your soul, if you are a believer in Christ Jesus. The Lord Jesus finished the work He came to do: do not tell Him that He did not. The Lord Jesus paid your debts in full: do not tell him that you think He left you to pay part. The Lord Jesus promises eternal life to every sinner that comes to Him: do not tell Him, even while you are coming, that you think He lies. Alas, for our unbelief! In Christ you are like Noah in the ark, and Lot in Zoar, nothing can harm you. The earth may be burned up with fire at the Lord's appearing, but not a hair of your head shall perish. Doubt it not. Pray for more faith. Watch and pray.

Watch against inconsistency of walk, and conformity to the world. Watch against sins of temper and of tongue. These are the kind of things that grieve the Spirit of God, and make His witness within us faint and low. Watch and pray.

Watch against the leaven of false doctrine. Remember that Satan can transform himself into an angel of light. Remember that bad money is never marked bad, or else it would never pass. Be very jealous for the whole truth as it is in Jesus. Do not put up with a grain of error merely for the sake of a pound of truth. Do not tolerate a little false doctrine one bit more than you would a little sin. Oh, reader, remember this caution! Watch and pray.

Watch against slothfulness about the Bible and private prayer. There is nothing so spiritual but we may at last do it formally. Most backslidings begin in the closet. When a tree is snapped in two by a high wind, we generally find there had been some long hidden decay. Oh, watch and pray!

Watch against bitterness and uncharitableness towards others. A little love is more valuable than many gifts. Be eagle-eyed in seeing the good that is in your brethren, and dim-sighted as the mole about the evil. Let your memory be a strong box for their graces, but a sieve for their faults. Watch and pray.

Watch against pride and self-conceit. Peter said at first, 'Though all men deny Thee, yet will not I.' And presently he fell. Pride is the high road to a fall. Watch and pray.

Watch against the sins of Galatia, Ephesus and Laodicea. Believers may run well for a season, then lose their first love and then become lukewarm. Watch and pray.

Watch not least against the sin of Jehu. A man may have great zeal to all appearance, and yet have very bad motives. It is a much easier thing to oppose AntiChrist than to follow Christ. It is one thing to protest against error; it is quite another thing to love the truth. So watch and pray.

Oh, my believing readers, let us all watch more than we have done! Let us watch more every year that we live. Let us watch, that we may not be startled when the Lord appears.

Let us watch *for the world's sake*. We are the books they chiefly read. They mark our ways far more than we think. Let us aim to be plainly-written epistles of Christ.

Let us watch *for our own sakes*. As our walk is, so will be our peace. As our conformity to Christ's mind, so will be our sense of Christ's atoning blood. If a man will not walk in the full light of the sun, how can he expect to be warm?

And, above all, let us watch *for our Lord Jesus Christ's sake*. Let us live as if His glory was concerned in our behaviour. Let us live as if every slip and fall was a reflection on the honour of our King. Let us live as if every allowed sin was one more thorn in His head, one more nail in His feet, one more spear in His side. Oh, let us exercise a godly jealousy over thoughts, words and actions, over motives, manners, and walk. Never, never let us fear being too strict. Never, never let us think we can watch too much. Leigh Richmond's dying words were very solemn. Few believers were ever more useful in their day and generation. Of few can it be said so truly, that he 'being dead yet speaketh'. But what did he say to one who stood by, while he lay dying?

'BROTHER, BROTHER, WE ARE NONE OF US MORE THAN HALF AWAKE!'

2

OCCUPY TILL I COME

And as they heard these things, he added and spake a parable, because he was nigh to Jerusalem, and because they thought that the kingdom of God should immediately appear. He said therefore, A certain nobleman went into a far country to receive for himself a kingdom, and to return. And he called his ten servants, and delivered them ten pounds, and said unto them, Occupy till I come (Luke 19:11-13).

The words before our eyes form an introduction to the parable, which is commonly called the 'Parable of the Pounds'. They contain matter which deserve the prayerful consideration of every true Christian in the present day.

There are some parables of which Matthew Henry says, with equal quaintness and truth, 'The key hangs beside the door.' The Holy Ghost Himself interprets them. There is no room left for doubt as to the purpose for which they were spoken. Of such parables the parable of the pounds is an example.

St. Luke tells us that our Lord Jesus Christ *added and spake a parable because he was night to Jerusalem, and because they thought that the kingdom of God should immediately appear.*

These words reveal to us the secret thoughts of our Lord's disciples at this period of His ministry. They were drawing night to Jerusalem. They gathered from many of their Master's sayings that something remarkable was about to happen. They had a strong impression that one great end of His coming into the world was about to be accomplished. So far they were quite right. As to the precise nature of the event about to happen they were quite wrong.

Reader, there are three subjects opened up in this passage of Scripture, which appear to me to be of the deepest importance. Upon each of these I wish to offer a few thoughts for your private meditation. I purposely abstain from touching any part of the parable except the beginning. I want to direct your attention to the three following points.

1. I will speak of the mistake of the disciples, referred to in the verses before us.

2. I will speak of the present position of the Lord Jesus Christ.

3. I will speak of the present duty of all who profess to be Jesus Christ's disciples.

May God bless the reading of this paper to everyone into whose hands it may fall. May every reader be taught to pray that the Spirit will guide him into all truth.

1. I will first speak of *the mistake into which the disciples had fallen.*

What was this mistake? Let us try to understand this point clearly. With what feelings ought Christians in the present day to regard this mistake? Let us try to understand this clearly also.

Our Lord's disciples seem to have thought that the Old Testament promises of Messiah's visible kingdom and glory were about to be immediately fulfilled. They believed rightly that he was indeed the Messiah, the Christ of God. But they blindly supposed that He was going at once to take to Himself His great power, and to reign gloriously over the earth. This was the sum and substance of their error.

They appear to have concluded that now was the day and now the hour when the Redeemer would build up Zion, and appear in His glory (Ps. 102:16); when He would smite the earth with the rod of His mouth, and with the breath of His lips slay the wicked; when He would assemble the outcasts of Israel, and gather the dispersed of Judah (Is. 11: 4, 12); when he would take the heathen for his inheritance, and the uttermost parts of the earth for His possession, break His enemies with a rod of iron, and dash them in pieces like a potter's vessel (Ps. 2: 8, 9); when He would reign in Mount Zion and in Jerusalem, and before his ancients gloriously (Is. 24:23); when the kingdom and dominion, and the greatness of the kingdom under the whole heaven would be given to the saints of the Most High (Dan. 7:27). Such appears to have been the mistake into which our Lord's disciples had fallen at the time when He spoke the parable of the pounds.

It was a *great mistake* unquestionably. They did not realise that before all these prophecies could be fulfilled, 'it behoved Christ to suffer' (Luke 24:46). Their sanguine expectations overleaped the crucifixion and the long parenthesis of time to follow, and bounded onward to the final glory. They did not see that there was to be a first advent of Messiah 'to be cut off', before the second advent of Messiah to reign. They did not perceive that the sacrifices and ceremonies of the law of Moses were first to receive their fulfilment in a better sacrifice and a better High Priest, and the shedding of blood more precious than that of bulls and goats. They did not comprehend that before the glory, Christ must be crucified, and an elect people gathered out from among the Gentiles by the preaching of the gospel. All these were dark things to them. They grasped part of the prophetical word, but not all. They saw that Christ was to have a kingdom, but they did not see that He was to be wounded and bruised, and be an offering for sin. They understood the end of the 2nd Psalm, and the whole of the 97th and 98th, but not the beginning of the 22nd. They understood the 11th chapter of Isaiah, but not the 53rd. They understood the dispensation of the crown and the glory, but not the dispensation of the cross and the shame. Such was their mistake.

It was a mistake which you will find partially *clinging to the disciples even after the crucifixion.* You see it creeping forth in the first days of the Church between the resurrection and the ascension. They said, 'Lord, wilt Thou at this time restore again the kingdom to Israel?'[2] (Acts 1:6). You find it referred to by St. Paul, 'Be not soon shaken in mind, or be troubled, neither by spirit, nor by word, nor by letter as from us, as that the day of Christ is at hand. Let no man deceive you by any means: for that day shall not come except there be a falling away first' (2 Thess. 2:2). In both these instances the old Jewish leaven peeps out. In both you see the same tendency to misunderstand God's purposes, to overlook the dispensation of the kingdom. In both you see the same disposition to neglect the duties of the present order of things. Those duties are: to bear the cross after Christ, to take part in the afflictions of the gospel, to work, to witness, to preach and to help to gather out a people for the Lord.

It was a mistake, however, which, I frankly say, I think we Gentile believers are bound to regard with much tenderness and consideration. It will not do to run down our Jewish brethren as 'carnal' and earthly-minded in their interpretation of prophecy, as if we Gentiles had never made any mistake at all. I think we have made great mistakes, and it is high time that we should confess it.

I believe we have fallen into an error parallel with that of our Jewish brethren, an error less fatal in its consequences than theirs, but an error far more inexcusable, because we have had more light. If the Jew thought too exclusively of Christ *reigning*, has not the Gentile thought too exclusively of

43

Christ *suffering*? If the Jew could see nothing in Old Testament prophecy but Christ's exaltation and final power, has not the Gentile often seen nothing but Christ's humiliation and the preaching of the gospel? If the Jew dwelt too much on Christ's *second* advent, has not the Gentile dwelt too exclusively on the *first*? If the Jew ignored the cross, has not the Gentile ignored the *crown*? I believe there can be but one answer to these questions. I believe that we Gentiles till lately have been very guilty concerning a large portion of God's truth. I believe that we have cherished an arbitrary, reckless habit of interpreting first advent texts *literally*, and second advent texts *spiritually*. I believe we have not rightly understood 'all that the prophets have spoken' about the second personal advent of Christ, any more than the Jews did about the first. And because we have done this, I say that we should speak of such mistakes as that referred to in our text with much tenderness and compassion.

Reader, I earnestly invite your special attention to the point on which I am now dwelling. I know not what your opinions may be about the fulfilment of the prohetical parts of Scripture. I approach the subject with fear and trembling, lest I should hurt the feelings of any dear brother in the Lord. But I ask you in all affection to examine your own views about prophecy. I am entreat you to consider calmly whether your opinions about Christ's second advent and kingdom are as sound and scriptural as those of His first disciples. I entreat you to take heed, lest insensibly you commit as great an error about Christ's second coming and glory as they did about Christ's first coming and cross.

I beseech you not to dismiss the subject which I now press upon your attention, as a matter of curious speculation, and one of no practical importance. Believe me, it affects the whole question between yourself and the unconverted Jew. I warn you that, unless you interpret the prophetical portion of the Old Testament in the simple literal meaning of its words, you will find it no easy matter to carry on an argument with an unconverted Jew.

You would probably tell the Jew that Jesus of Nazareth was the Messiah promised in the Old Testament Scriptures. To those Scriptures you would refer him for proof. You would show him Psalm 22, Isaiah 53, Daniel 9:26, Micah 5:2, Zechariah 9:9 and 11:13. You would tell him that in Jesus of Nazareth those Scriptures were literally fulfilled. You would urge upon him that he ought to believe these Scriptures, and receive Christ as the Messiah. All this is very good. So far you would do well.

But suppose the Jew asks you if you take *all* the prophecies of the Old Testament in their simple literal meaning. Suppose he asks you if you believe in a literal personal advent of Messiah to reign over the earth in glory, a literal restoration of Judah and Israel to Palestine, a literal rebuilding and restoration of Zion and Jerusalem. Suppose the unconverted Jew puts these questions to you, what answer are you prepared to make?

Will you dare to tell him that Old Testament prophecies of this kind are not to be taken in their plain literal sense? Will you dare to tell him that the words Zion, Jerusalem, Jacob, Judah, Ephraim, Israel, do not mean what they seem to mean, but mean the *Church of Christ?* Will you dare to tell him that the glorious kingdom and future blessedness of Zion, so often dwelt upon in prophecy, mean nothing more than the gradual Christianising of the world by missionaries and gospel preaching? Will you dare to tell him that you think it 'carnal' to take such Scriptures literally, 'carnal' to expect a literal rebuilding of Jerusalem, 'carnal' to expect a literal coming of Messiah to reign, 'carnal' to look for a literal gathering and restoration of Israel? Oh, reader, if you are a man of this mind, take care what you are doing! I say again, take care.

Do you not see that you are putting a weapon in the hand of the unconverted Jew, which he will probably use with irresistible power? Do you not see that you are cutting the ground from under your own feet, and supplying the Jew with a strong argument for not believing your own interpretation of Scripture? Do you not see that the Jew will reply, that it is 'carnal' to tell him that the Messiah *has* come literally to *suffer*, if you tell him that it is 'carnal' to expect Messiah *will* come *literally* to *reign?* Do you not see that the Jew will tell you, that it is far more 'carnal' in you to believe that Messiah could come into the world as a despised, crucified Man of sorrows, than it is in him to believe that He will come into the world as a glorious King? Beyond doubt he will do so, and you will find no answer to give.

Reader, I commend these things to your serious attention. I entreat you to throw aside all prejudice, and to view the subject I am dwelling upon with calm and dispassionate thought. I beseech you to take up anew the prophetical Scriptures, and to pray that you may not err in interpreting their meaning. Read them in the light of those two great polestars, the first and second advents of Jesus Christ. Bind up with the *first advent* the rejection of the Jews, the calling of the Gentiles, the preaching of the gospel as a witness to the world and the gathering out of the election of grace. Bind up with the *second advent* the restoration of the Jews, the pouring out of judgments on unbelieving Christians, the conversion of the world and the establishment of Christ's kingdom upon earth. Do this and you will see a meaning and fullness in prophecy which perhaps you have never yet discovered.

I am quite aware that many good men do not see the subject of unfulfilled prophecy as I do. I am painfully sensible that I seem presumptuous in differing from them. But I dare not refuse anything which appears to me plainly written in Scripture. I consider the best of men are not infallible. I think we should remember that we must reject Protestant traditions which are not according to the Bible, as much as the traditions of the Church of Rome.

I believe it is high time for the Church of Christ to awake out of its sleep about Old Testament prophecy. From the time of the Old Fathers, Jerome and Origen, down to the present day, men have gone on in a pernicious habit of 'spiritualising' the words of the Prophets, until their true meaning has been well nigh buried. It is high time to lay aside traditional methods of interpretation, and to give up our blind obedience to the opinions of such writers as Poole, Henry, Scott and Clarke, upon unfulfilled prophecy. It is high time to fall back on the good old principle that Scripture generally means what it seems to mean, and to beware of that semi-sceptical argument, *'Such and such an interpretation cannot be correct, because it seems to us "carnal"!'*

It is high time for Christians to interpret unfulfilled prophecy *by the light of prophecies already fulfilled.* The curses on the Jews were brought to pass literally: so also will be the blessings. The scattering was literal: so also will be the gathering. The pulling down of Zion was literal: so also will be the building up. The rejection of Israel was literal: so also will be the restoration.

It is high time to interpret the events that shall accompany Christ's second advent *by the light of those accompanying His first advent.* The first advent was literal, visible, personal: so also will be His second. His first advent was with a literal body: so also will be His second. At His first advent the least predictions were fulfilled to the very letter: so also will they be at His second. The shame was literal and visible: so also will be the glory.

It is high time to cease from explaining Old Testament prophecies *in a way not warranted by the New Testament.* What right have we to say that the words Judah, Zion, Israel and Jerusalem, ever mean anything but literal Judah, literal Zion, literal Israel and literal Jerusalem? What precedent shall we find in the New Testament? Hardly any, if indeed any at all. Well says an admirable writer on this subject:

There are really only two or three places in the whole New Testament, Gospels, Epistles and Revelation, where such names are used decidedly in what may be called a spiritual or figurative state. The word 'Jerusalem' occurs eighty times, and all of them unquestionably literal, save when the opposite is expressly pointed out by epithets, 'heavenly' or 'new' or 'holy'. 'Jew' occurs an hundred times, and only four are even ambiguous, as Rom. 2:28. 'Israel' and 'Israelite' occur forty times, and all literal. 'Judah' and 'Judea' above twenty times, and all literal (Horatius Bonar, *Prophetical Landmarks*, p 300).

It is no answer to all this to tell us that it is impossible to carry out the principle of a literal interpretation, and that Christ was not a literal 'door', nor a literal 'branch', nor the bread in the sacrament His literal 'body'. I reply that when I speak of literal interpretation, I require no man to deny the use of *figurative* language. I fully admit that emblems, figures and symbols are used in foretelling Messiah's glory, as well as in foretelling Messiah's sufferings. I do not believe that Jesus was a literal 'root out of dry ground' or a literal 'lamb' (Isa. 53). All I maintain is, that prophecies about Christ's coming and kingdom do foretell literal facts as truly as the prophecy about Christ being 'numbered with the transgressors'. All I say is, that prophecies about the Jews being gathered will be as really and literally made good as those about the Jews being scattered.

It is no good argument to tell us that the principle of literal interpretation deprives the Church of the use and benefit of many parts of the Old Testament. I deny the justice of the charge altogether. I consider that all things written in the Prophets concerning the salvation of individual souls may be used by Gentiles as freely as by Jews. The hearts of Jews and Gentiles are naturally just the same. The way to heaven is but one. Both Jews and Gentiles need justification, regeneration, sanctification. Whatever is written concerning such subjects, is just as much the property of the Gentile as the Jew. Moreover, I hold Israel to be a people specially typical of the whole body of believers in Christ. I consider that believers now may take the comfort of every promise of pardon, comfort and grace which is addressed to Israel. Such words I regard as the common portion of all believers. All I maintain is, that whenever God says He shall do or give certain things to Israel and Jerusalem *in this world* we ought entirely to believe that to literal Israel and Jerusalem those things will be given and done.

It is no valid argument to say that many who think as I do about prophecy have said and written very foolish things, and have often contradicted one another. All this may be very true, and yet the *principles* for which we contend may be scriptural, sound and correct. The infidel does not overturn the truth of Christianity when he points to the existence of Antinomians, Jumpers and Shakers. The worldly man does not overturn the truth of real evangelical religion when he sneers at the differences of Calvinists and Arminians. Just in the same way one writer on prophecy may interpret Revelation or Daniel in one way, and another in another. One man may take on him to fix dates, and prove at last to be quite wrong. Another may apply prophecies to living individuals, and prove utterly mistaken. But all these things do not affect the main question. They do not in the least prove that the advent of Christ *before* the millennium is not a scriptural truth, and that the principle of interpreting Old Testament prophecy *literally* is not a sound principle.

Reader, I say once more, we ought to regard the mistakes of our Lord's disciples with great tenderness and consideration. We Christians are the last who ought to condemn them strongly. Great as their mistakes were, our own have been almost as bad. We have been very quick in discovering the beam in our Jewish brother's eyes, and have forgotten a large mote in our own. We have been long putting a great stumbling-block in his way, by our arbitrary and inconsistent explanations of Old Testament prophecy.

Reader, let us do our part to remove that great stumbling-block. If we would help to remove the veil which prevents the Jews seeing the *cross*, let us also strip off the veil from our own eyes and look steadily and unflinchingly *at the second advent and the crown.*[3]

2. The second question I wish to consider is this: *What is the present position of our Lord Jesus Christ?*

The parable appears to me to answer that question distinctly in the twelfth verse. 'A certain nobleman went into a far country to receive for himself a kingdom, and to return.'

This nobleman represents the Lord Jesus Christ, and that in two respects. Like the nobleman, the Lord Jesus is gone into a far country to receive for Himself a kingdom. *He has not received it yet in possession,* though He has it in promise. He has a spiritual kingdom unquestionably. He is King over the hearts of His believing people, and they are all His faithful subjects. He has a controlling power over the world without controversy. He is King of kings and Lord of lords. 'By Him all things consist', and nothing can happen without His permission. But his real, literal, visible, complete kingdom the Lord Jesus has not yet received. To use the words of Hebrews 2:8 'We see not yet all things put under Him'. To use the words of Psalm 110:1, 'He sits on the right hand of the Father till His enemies are made His footstool.'

The devil is the prince of this world during the present dispensation (John 14:30). The vast majority of the inhabitants of the earth choose the things that please the devil far more than the things that please God. Little as they may think it, they are doing the devil's will, behaving as the devil's subjects, and serving the devil, far more than Christ. This is the actual condition of Christendom as well as of heathen countries. After 1,800 years of Bibles and gospel preaching, there is not a nation, or a country, or a parish, or a long-established congregation, where the devil has not more subjects than Christ. So fearfully true is it that the world is not yet the kingdom of Christ.

The Lord Jesus during the present dispensation is like David between the time of his anointing and Saul's death. He has the promise of the kingdom, but He has not yet received the crown and throne (1 Sam. 22:1, 2).

He is followed by a few, and those often neither great nor wise; but they are a faithful people. He is persecuted by His enemies, and oft times driven into the wilderness; and yet His party is never quite destroyed. But He has none of the visible signs of the kingdom at present, no earthly glory, majesty, greatness, obedience. The vast majority of mankind see no beauty in Him. They will not have this Man to reign over them. His people are not honoured for their Master's sake. They walk the earth like princes in disguise. His kingdom is not yet come. His will is not yet done on earth, excepting by a little flock. It is not the day of *His power*. The Lord Jesus is biding His time.

Reader, I entreat you to grasp firmly this truth, for truth I believe it to be. Great delusion abounds on the subject of Christ's kingdom. Take heed lest any man deceive you by purely traditional teachings about prophetical truth. Hymns are composed and sung which darken God's counsel on this subject by words without knowledge. Texts are wrested from their true meaning, and accommodated to the present order of things, which are not justly applicable to any but the period of the second advent. Beware of the mischievous infection of this habit of text wresting. Beware of the sapping and mining effect of beautiful poetry in which unfulfilled promises of glory are twisted and adapted to the present dispensation. Settle it down in your mind that Christ's kingdom is yet to come. His arrows are not yet sharp in the hearts of His enemies. The day of His power has not yet begun. He is gathering out a people to carry the cross and walk in His steps. But the time of His coronation has not yet arrived. But just as the Lord Jesus, like the nobleman, 'went to receive a kingdom'; so like the nobleman, the Lord Jesus intends one day 'to return'.

The words of the angels shall have a complete fulfilment, 'This same Jesus which was taken from you into heaven, shall so come in like manner as ye have seen Him go into heaven' (Acts 1:11). As His going away was a real literal going away, so His return shall be a real literal return. As He came personally the first time with a body, so He shall come personally the second time with a body. As He came visibly to this earth and visibly went away, so when he comes the second time He shall visibly return. And then, and not till then, the complete kingdom of Christ shall begin. He left His servants as a 'nobleman'; He returns to His servants as a 'king'.

Then He intends to cast out that old usurper the devil, to bind him for a thousand years, and to strip him of his power (Rev. 20:1).

Then He intends to make a restitution of the face of creation (Acts 3:21). It shall be the world's jubilee day. Our earth shall at last bring forth her increase. The King shall at length have His own again. At last the 97th Psalm shall be fulfilled, and men shall say, 'The Lord reigneth: let the earth rejoice!'

Then He intends to fulfil the prophecies of Enoch, John the Baptist and St. Paul, 'To execute judgment upon all the ungodly' inhabitants of Christendom, 'to burn up the chaff with unquenchable fire' and 'in flaming fire to take vengeance on them that know not God, and obey not the Gospel' (Jude 15; Matt. 3:12; 2 Thess. 1:8).

Then He intends to raise His dead saints and gather His living ones, to gather together the scattered tribes of Israel, and to set up an empire on earth in which every knee shall bow to Him, and every tongue confess that Christ is the Lord.

When, how, where, in what manner, all these things shall be, we cannot say particularly. Enough for us to know that *they shall be*. The Lord Jesus waits for the time to do them, and they shall be performed. The Lord Jesus waits for the time appointed by the Father, and then shall they all come to pass. As surely as He was born of a pure virgin, and lived on earth thirty-three years as a servant, so surely He shall come with clouds in glory, and reign on the earth as a king.

Reader, I charge you to establish in your mind among the great verities of your religion, that Christ is one day to have a complete kingdom in this world, that His kingdom is not yet set up, but that it will be set up in the day of His return. Know clearly whose kingdom it is now: not Christ's, but the usurper Satan's. Know clearly whose kingdom it is to be one day: not Satan the usurper's, but Jesus Christ's. Know clearly when the kingdom is to change hands, and the usurper to be cast out: when the Lord Jesus returns in person, and not before. Know clearly what the Lord Jesus is doing now: He is sitting at the right hand of the Father, interceding as a High Priest in the holy of holies for His people, adding to their number such as shall be saved by the preaching of the gospel, and waiting till the appointed 'day of His power', when He shall come forth to bless His people, and sit as a 'priest upon His throne' (Zech. 6:13). Know these things clearly and you will do well.

Know these things clearly, and then *you will not cherish extravagant expectations* from any church, minister or religious machinery in this present dispensation. You will not marvel to see ministers and missionaries not converting all to whom they preach. You will not wonder to find that while some believe the gospel, many believe not. You will not be depressed and cast down when you see the children of the world in every place many, and the children of God few. You will remember that 'the days are evil' and that the time of general conversion has not yet arrived. You will thank God that any are converted at all, and that while the gospel is hid to the wise and prudent, it is yet revealed to babes. Alas, for the man who expects a millennium before the Lord Jesus returns! How can this possibly be, if the world in the day of His coming is to be found as it was in the days of Noah and Lot? (Luke 17:28-30).

Know these things clearly, and then *you will not be confounded and surprised by the continuance of immense evils in the world.* Wars, and tumults, and oppression, and dishonesty, and selfishness, and covetousness, and superstition, and bad government, and abounding heresies, will not appear to you unaccountable. You will not sink down into a morbid, misanthropic condition of mind, when you see laws, and reforms, and education, not making mankind perfect. You will not relapse into a state of apathy and disgust when you see churches full of imperfections and theologians making mistakes. You will say to yourself, 'The time of Christ's power has not yet arrived, the devil is still working among his children, and sowing darkness and division broadcast among the saints, the true King is yet to come.'

Know these things clearly, and then *you will see why God delays the final glory*, and allows things to go as they do in this world. It is not that He is not able to prevent evil, it is not that He is slack in the fulfilling of His promises, but the Lord is taking out for Himself a people by the preaching of the gospel (Acts 15:14; 2 Peter 3:9). He is longsuffering to unconverted Christians. 'The Lord is not willing that any should perish, but that all should come to repentance.' Once let the number of the elect be gathered out of the world, once let the last elect sinner be brought to repentance, and then the kingdom of Christ shall be set up, and the throne of grace shall be exchanged for the throne of glory.

Know these things clearly, and then *you will work diligently to do good to souls*. The time is short. 'The night is far spent. The day is at hand.' The signs of the times call loudly for watchfulness, and speak with no uncertain voice. The Turkish empire is drying up. The Jews are cared for as they never have been for eighteen hundred years. The gospel is being preached as a witness in almost every corner of the world. Surely if we would pluck a few more brands from the burning before it is too late, we must work hard and lose no time. We must preach, we must warn, we must exhort, we must give money to religious societies, we must spend and be spent far more than we have ever done yet.

Know these things clearly, and then you *will be often looking for the coming of the day of God*. you will regard the second advent as a glorious and comfortable truth, around which your best hopes will all be clustered. You will not merely think of Christ crucified, but you will think also of Christ coming again. You will long for the days of refreshing and the manifestation of the sons of God (Acts 3:19; Rom. 8:19). You will find peace in looking back to the cross, and you will find joyful hope in looking forward to the kingdom.

Once more, I repeat, now clearly Christ's present position. He is like one who is 'gone into a far country to receive a kingdom and then to return'.

3. The third and last question I wish to consider is this: *What is the present duty of all Christ's professing disciples?*
When I speak of present duty, I mean of course their duty between the period of Christ's first and second advents. And I find an answer in the words of the nobleman, in the parable to his servants: 'he delivered them ten pounds, and said unto them, Occupy till I come.'

Reader, I know few words more searching and impressive than these four 'Occupy till I come'. They are spoken to all who profess and call themselves Christians. They address the conscience of every one who has not renounced his baptism, and formally turned his back on Christianity. They ought to stir up all hearers of the gospel to examine themselves whether they are in the faith, and to prove themselves. Listen to me for a few minutes, while I try to impress them on your attention. For your sake, remember, these words were written: 'Occupy till I come.'

The Lord Jesus bids you *'occupy'*. By that He means that you are to be a 'doer' in your Christianity, and not merely a hearer and professor. He wants His servants not only to receive His wages, and eat His bread, and dwell in His house, and belong to His family, but also to do His work. You are to 'let your light so shine before men that they may see your good works' (Matt. 5:16). Have you faith? It must not be a dead faith: 'it must work by love' (Gal. 5:6). Are you elect? You are elect unto 'obedience' (1 Peter 1:2). Are you redeemed? You are redeemed that you may be a 'peculiar people, zealous of good works' (Titus 2:14). Do you love Christ? Prove the reality of your love by keeping Christ's commandments (John 14:15). Oh, reader, do not forget this charge to 'occupy. Beware of an idle, talking, gossiping, sentimental, do-nothing religion. Think not because your doings cannot justify you, or put away one single sin, that therefore it matters not whether you do anything at all. Away with such a delusion! Cast it behind you as an invention of the devil. Think of the house built upon the sand, and its miserable end (Matt. 7:24-27). As ever you would 'make your calling and election sure', be a doing Christian.

But the Lord Jesus also bids you *occupy your pound*. By this He means that He has given each one of His people some opportunity of glorifying Him. He would have you understand that every one has got his own sphere, the poorest as well as the richest, that every one has an open door before him, and may, if he will, show forth his Master's praise. Your bodily health and strength, your mental gifts and capacities, your money and your earthly possessions, your rank and position in life, your example and influence with others, your liberty to read the Bible and hear the gospel, your plentiful supply of means of grace, all these are your 'pounds'. All these are to be used and employed with a continual reference to the glory of Christ. All these are His gifts. 'Of Him come riches and honour' (1 Chron. 29:12). 'His is the silver, and His is the gold' (Hagg. 2:8). 'His is your body and His is your spirit' (1 Cor. 6:20). 'He appoints your habitation. He gives you life and breath' (Acts 17: 25, 26). 'You are not your own. You are bought with a price' (1 Cor. 6:20). Surely it is no great matter if He bids you honour Him and serve Him with all that you have. Breathes there the man or woman among the readers of this paper who has received nothing at the Lord's hand? Not one, I am sure. Oh! see to it, that you lay out your Lord's money well and honestly! Take heed that you do not bury your pound!

But the Lord Jesus bids you also to *occupy till He comes*. By that He means that you are to do His work on earth, like one who continually looks for His return. You are to be like the faithful servant, who knows not what hour his master may come home, but keeps all things in readiness, and is always prepared. You are to be like one who knows that Christ's coming is the great reckoning day, and to be ready to render up your account at any moment. You are not to suppose that you have any freehold in this world, nor even a lease. The greatest and the richest of mankind is only God's tenant will. You are not to neglect any social duty or relation of life because of the uncertainty of the Lord's return. You are to fill the station to which God has called you in a godly and Christian way; and you are to be ready to go from the place of business to meet Christ in the air, if the Lord shall think fit. You are to be like a man who never knows what a day might bring forth, and, therefore, you are to put off nothing till a 'convenient season'. You are to rise and go forth in the morning ready, if need be, to meet Christ at noon. You are to lie down in bed at night ready, if need be, to be awakened by the midnight cry, 'Behold the Bridegroom cometh.' You are to keep your spiritual accounts in a state of constant preparation, like one who never knows how soon they may be called for. You are to measure all your ways by the measure of Christ's appearing, and to do nothing in which you would not like Jesus to find you engaged. This is to 'occupy' till Jesus comes.

Think, reader, how *condemning* are these words to thousands of professing Christians! What an utter absence of preparation appears in their daily walk and conversation! How thoroughly unfit they are to meet Christ! They know nothing of occupying the gifts of God as loans for which they must give account. They show not the slightest desire to glorify Him with 'body and spirit, which are His'. They give no sign of readiness for the second advent. Well says old Gurnall, 'It may be written on the grave of every unconverted man, Here lies one who never did for God an hour's work.' Who can wonder in a world like this, if a minister often cries to his congregation, 'Ye must be born again'; 'Except ye be converted, and become as little children, ye shall not enter into the kingdom of heaven' (John 3:7; Matt. 18:3).

Think again, how *arousing* these words ought to be to all who are rich in this world, but do not know how to spend their money rightly. Alas! there are many who live on as if Christ had never said anything about the difficulty of rich men being saved. They are rich towards their own pleasures, of their own tastes, or their own families, but not rich towards God! They live as if they would not have to give an account of their use of money. They live as if there was no reckoning day before the bar of Christ. They live as if Christ had never said 'It is more blessed to give than to receive' (Acts 20:35). 'Sell that ye have and give alms. Provide yourselves bags which wax not old, a treasure in heaven that faileth not' (Luke 12:33). Oh! if this paper should by chance fall into the hands of such a one, I do beseech you, consider your ways and be wise. Cease to be content with giving God's cause a few shillings, or an occasional guinea. Give far more liberally than you have done, yet. Give hundreds where you now give tens. Give thousands where you now give hundreds. Then, and not till then, I shall believe you are 'occupying' as one who looks for Christ's return. Alas, for the covetousness and narrow-mindedness of the Church these days! May the Lord open the eyes of rich Christians.

Think again, how *instructive* are these words to all who are troubled by doubts about mingling with the world, and taking part in its vain amusements. It is useless to tell us that races, and balls, and theatres, and operas, and cards, are not *forbidden* by name in Scripture. The question we should ask ourselves is simply this, 'Am I occupying as one who looks for Christ's return, when I take part in these things? Should I like Jesus to return suddenly and find me on the racecourse, or in the ballroom, or at the theatre, or at the card-table? Should I think I was in my right place, and where my Lord would have me to be?' Oh, dear reader, this is the true test by which to try all our daily occupations and employments of time! That *thing* which we would not do if we thought Jesus was coming tonight, that thing we ought not to do at all. That *place* to which we would not go if we thought Jesus was coming this day, that place we ought to avoid. That *company* in which we would not like Jesus to find us, in that company we ought never to sit down. Oh, that men would live as in the sight of Christ! Not as in the sight of man, or of the church, or of ministers, but as in the sight of Christ! This would be 'occupying till He comes'.

But think how *encouraging* are these words to all who seek first the kingdom of God, and love the Lord Christ in sincerity. What though the children of the world regard them as 'righteous over much'! What though mistaken friends and relations tell them they pay too much attention to religion, and go too far! Those words, 'Occupy till I come', are words which justify their conduct. They may well reply to their persecutors, 'I am doing a great work, and I cannot come down; I am striving to live so as to be ready when the Lord comes; I must be about my Father's business.'

Let me conclude this address by a few words of general application.

1. First, let me draw from the whole subject a word of *solemn warning* for every one into whose hands this address may fall. That warning is, that there

is a great change yet to come on this world, and a change we ought to keep constantly before our mind's eye.

That change is a change of *masters*. That old rebel, the devil, and all his adherents, shall be cast down. The Lord Jesus, and all His saints, shall be exalted and raised to honour. 'The kingdoms of this world' shall 'become the kingdoms of our Lord, and of His Christ' (Rev. 11:15).

That change is a change of *manners*. Sin shall no longer be made light of and palliated. Wickedness shall no longer go unpunished and unreproved. Holiness shall become the general character of the inhabitants of the earth. 'The new heaven and new earth' shall be the dwelling of 'righteousness' (2 Peter 3:13).

That change is a change of *opinion*. There shall be no more Socinianism, or Deism, or Scepticism, or Infidelity. All nations shall do honour to the crucified Lamb of God. All men shall know him, from the least to the greatest. 'The earth shall be full of the knowledge of Him, as the waters cover the sea' (Isa. 11:9).

I say nothing as to the time when these things shall take place. I object, on principle, to all dogmatism about dates. All I insist upon is this, that there is a great change before us all, a change for the earth, a change for man, and, above all, a change for the saints.

I accept the prediction that *there is a great improvement and development of human nature yet to take place*. I accept it with all my heart. But how and when shall it be brought about? Not by any system of education! Not by any legislation of politicians! Not by anything short of the appearing of the kingdom of Christ. Then, and then only, shall there be universal justice, universal knowledge and universal peace.

I accept the common phrase of many. *There is a good time coming*. I accept it with all my heart. I do verily believe there shall one day be no more poverty, no more oppression, no more ignorance, no more grinding competition, no more covetousness. But when shall that good time come? Never! never till the return of Jesus Christ at His second advent. And for whom shall that time be good? For none but those who know and love the Lord.

I accept the common phrase, *There is a man coming who will set all right that now is wrong. We wait for the coming man*. I accept it with all my heart. I do look for One who shall unravel the tangled skein of this world's affairs, and put everything in its right place. But who is the great Physician for an old, diseased, worn-out world? It is 'the man Christ Jesus', who is yet to return.

Oh, reader, let us realise this point! There is before us all a great change. Surely, when a man has notice to quit his present dwelling place, he ought to make sure that he has before him another home.

2. Next, let me draw from the whole subject a solemn question for all into whose hands this address may fall. That question is simply this, ARE YOU READY FOR THE GREAT CHANGE? Are you ready for the coming and kingdom of Christ? Remember, I do not ask what you think about controversial points in the subject of prophecy. I do not ask your opinion about preterism and futurism. I do not ask whether you think revelation fulfilled or unfulfilled, or whether you consider the Man of Sin to be an individual, or whether you hold prophetical days to be years. About all these points you and I may err, and yet be saved. The one point to which I want to fix you down is this: 'Are you ready for the kingdom of Christ?'

It is useless to tell me that, in asking this, I put before you too high a standard. It is vain to tell me that a man may be a very good man, and yet not be ready for the kingdom of Christ. I deny it altogether. I say that every justified and converted man is ready, and that if you are not ready you are not a justified man. I say that the standard I put before you is nothing more than the New Testament standard, and the Apostles would have doubted the truth of your religion, if you were not looking and longing for the coming of the Lord. I say above all that the grand end of the gospel is to prepare men to meet God. What has your Christianity done for you if it has not made you meet for the kingdom of Christ? Nothing! nothing at all! Oh, that you may think on this matter, and never rest till you are ready to meet Christ!

3. In the next place let me offer *an invitation* to all readers who do not feel ready for Christ's return. That invitation shall be short and simple. I beseech you to know your danger, and come to Christ without delay, that you may be pardoned, justified and made ready for things to come. I entreat you this day to 'flee from the wrath to come', to the hope set before you in the gospel. 'I pray you in Christ's stead, to lay down enmity and unbelief, and at once to be reconciled to God' (2. Cor. 5:20).

I tremble when I think of the privileges which surround you in this country, and of the peril in which you stand so long as you neglect them. I tremble when I think of the possibility of Christ coming again, and of your being found unpardoned and unconverted in the day of His return. Better a thousand times will be his lot who was born a heathen, and never heard the gospel, than the lot of him who has been a member of a church, but not a living member of Christ. Surely the time past may suffice you to have delayed and lingered about your soul. Awake this day! 'Awake thou that sleepest, and Christ shall give thee light' (Eph. 5:14).

Lay aside everything that stands between you and Christ. Cast away everything that draws you back and prevents you feeling ready for the Lord's appearing. Find out the besetting sin that weighs you down, and tear it from your heart, however dear it may be. Cry mightily to the Lord Jesus to reveal Himself to your soul. Rest not till you have got a real, firm and reasonable hope, and know that your feet are on the Rock of Ages. Rest not till you can say, 'The Lord may come; the earth may be shaken; the foundations of the round world may be overturned; but thank God I have got treasure in heaven, and an Advocate with the Father, and I will not be afraid.'
Do this, and you shall have got something from reading a simple prophetical paper.

4. Last of all, let me draw from the subject *an exhortation* to all who know Christ indeed, and love His appearing. That exhortation is simply this, that you will strive more and more to be a 'doing' Christian (James 1:22). Labour more and more to show forth the praises of Him who hath called you out of darkness into marvellous light. Improve every talent which the Lord Jesus has committed to your charge to the setting forth of His glory. Let your walk declare plainly that you 'seek a country'. Let you conformity to the mind of Christ be unquestionable and unmistakable. Let you holiness be a clear plain fact, which even the worst enemies of the gospel cannot deny.

Above all, if you are a student of prophecy, I entreat you never to let it be said that prophetical study prevents practical diligence. If you do believe that the day is really approaching, then labour actively to provoke others unto love and good works. If you do believe that the night is far spent, be doubly diligent to 'cast off the works of darkness and put on the armour of light'. Never was there a greater mistake than to fancy the doctrine of the personal return of Christ is calculated to paralyse Christian diligence. Surely there can be no greater spur to the servant's activity than the expectation of His master's speedy return.

This is the way to attain a *healthy* state of soul. There is nothing like the exercises of our graces for promoting our spiritual vigour. Alas, there are not a few of God's saints who complain that they want spiritual comfort in their religion, while the fault is altogether in themselves. 'OCCUPY, OCCUPY',

I would say to such persons. Lay yourselves out more heartily for the glory of God and these uncomfortable feelings will soon vanish away.

This is the way to *do good* to the children of the world. Nothing, under God, has such an effect on unconverted people as the sight of a real, thoroughgoing live Christian. there are thousands who will not come to hear the gospel, and do not know the meaning of justification by faith, who yet can understand an uncompromising, holy, consistent walk with God. 'OCCUPY, OCCUPY', I say again, if you want to do good.

This is the way to promote *meetness* for the inheritance of the saints in light. There will be no idleness in the kingdom of Christ. The saints and angels shall there wait on their Lord with unwearied activity, and serve Him day and night. It is a fine saying of Bernard, that Jacob in his vision saw some angels ascending, and some descending, but none standing still. 'OCCUPY, OCCUPY,' I say again, if you would be thoroughly trained for your glorious home.

Oh, brethren believers, it would be well indeed if we did but see clearly how much it is for our interest and happiness to occupy every farthing of our Lord's money, to live very near to God.

So living we shall find great joy in our work, great comfort in our trials, great doors of usefulness in the world, great consolation in our sicknesses, great hope in our death, leave great evidences behind us when we are buried, have great confidence in the day of Christ's return and receive a great crown in the day of reward.

3

WHAT TIME IS IT?

The night is far spent, the day is at hand: let us therefore cast off the works of darkness, and let us put on the armour of light (Rom. 13:12).

You probably know the story of St. Paul's shipwreck (Acts 28). You remember how the Apostle and his companions were exceedingly tossed with a tempest for thirteen days. Neither sun nor stars in many days appeared. All hope that they should be saved was taken away. But do you recollect that when the fourteenth night was come, about midnight, the shipmen deemed that they drew near to some country? They sounded, and found it twenty fathoms. When they had gone a little further they sounded again, and found it fifteen fathoms. Then, fearing lest they should have fallen upon rocks, they cast four anchors out of the stern, and wished for the day. Think what an anxious night that must have been! How often some of the two hundred and seventy-six souls on board the great Alexandrian corn ship must have said, How goes the night? *What time is it?*

You have probably heard of the battle of Waterloo. You know that the Duke of Wellington fought that battle on the understanding that the Prussians would come upon the left of his army, and help him against the French. But the way was long. The roads were bad. The evening was drawing on before the Prussians could appear on the field. In the meantime the battle increased. Hour after hour our forces were thinned by the furious attacks of the enemy. One gallant man after another was slain or carried away wounded. Think what an anxious afternoon that must have been! How often the sun and shadows must have been observed! How often the watch must have been consulted, and the general's eye turned to the left! How often the anxious question must have risen in men's minds, *What time is it?*

You have probably attended the sickbed of some whom you tenderly loved. You have seen them hovering between life and death, and have passed weeks of painful suspense. You have sat by and watched the struggle between the body and its infirmities, and felt the miserable helplessness of not being able to do anything but look on. And do you not know how slowly the hours roll round at a time like this? Have not the clocks and watches seemed to stand still, and the sun appeared to have forgotten to rise? Have you not often said, When will the physician come again? Will the morning never come? *What time is it?*

Reader, you and I are in a world which is rapidly rolling on towards the day of judgment. There is an hour before us all when the earth and its works shall be burned up, and the inhabitants thereof shall all stand before the bar of Christ. There is a day to come whose issues are of far more importance than those of shipwreck, battle or disease. Surely it becomes us to think of that day. Are we ready for it? Is it possible that we may live to see it? Is it near, or is it far off? *What time is it?*

Come with me this day and consider the thoughts of an inspired Apostle on this solemn subject. He says, 'The night is far spent, the day is at hand: Let us therefore cast off the works of darkness and let us put on the armour of light.' These words ought to come home to our consciences like the blast of a trumpet. They ought to rouse our sleeping minds to a sense of the eternal realities which are before us. They call upon us to lay aside all trifling, lingering and carelessness about our Christianity. They summon us to a close walk with God.

There are four things brought before my mind by the words just quoted.

1. You have here *the present condition of the world* : it is night.

2. You have *the condition of the world which is yet to come:* it will be day.

3. You have *the particular time in which our lot is cast:* the night is far spent and the day is at hand.

4. You have *the duty of all believers who know the time:* they ought to cast off the works of darkness, and to put on the armour of light. Upon each of these four points I have something to say.

1. First of all let us consider the present condition of the world.

The Apostle Paul calls it 'night'. 'The night', he says, 'is far spent.' I have no doubt that word seems strange to some persons. They think it wonderful that the year 1879 should be called 'night'. They are living in days of learning, science, civilisation, commerce, freedom and knowledge. They see around them things which their forefathers never dreamed of – railways, manufactories, gas, electricity, steam engines, education for all and cheap books. I know it all, and am thankful for it. Nevertheless I say that in the things of God the world is still in a state of 'night'.

I believe that God looks down on this globe of ours as it rolls round the sun, and as He looks upon it, He pronounces it 'very dark'.

I believe that the angels go to and fro, and make report of all they see on our earth, and their constant report is 'very dark'.

And I am sure that believers in the Lord Jesus in every land are of one mind on this subject. They cry and sigh for the abominations they see around them. To them the world appears 'very dark'.

Is it not dark in *heathen lands?* There are two-thirds of the whole world in open rebellion against God and His Christ. Two out of every three inhabitants of the globe have no Bible, no gospel, no knowledge, no faith, no hope. They are cruel, deceitful, immoral, unclean, earthly, sensual, devilish, idolatrous, superstitious. Surely that is night.

Is it not dark *in many professedly Christian countries?* There are two-thirds of all the professing Christians on earth who are unsound in the faith. Their religion is not simply scriptural. They have added to it many things which are not to be found in the Bible. They have left out of it many things which the Bible has plainly commanded. There are millions who give honour to the Virgin Mary and dead saints instead of Christ. There are millions of baptised people who know nothing of the Bible, and have not the slightest idea of the salvation contained in the gospel. Surely that is night.

Is it not dark in *our own country* at this present day? How much of sin there is in Protestant Britain, and how little of God! How much of open infidelity, heathenish, ignorance, drunkenness, Sabbath-breaking, swearing, cheating, lying, covetousness, is weekly crying against us before the Lord of Hosts! How many people in Great Britain go to no place of worship at all! How many go to church and chapel merely as a matter of form! How few are really in earnest about the salvation of their souls! How few have any evidence to show of a saving faith in Christ, and a real work of the Spirit in their hearts! Surely even among ourselves it is night.

Is there not *much darkness under the eyes of every true believer?* Go to the most godly, quiet and orderly parish in our land at this moment. Ask any well-informed child of God residing in it, how many true Christians it contains, and what is the proportion of the converted to the unconverted. Mark well the answer he will give. I doubt if you find a parish in Great Britain where one-third of the people are converted. And if such be the report of parishes which are like the green tree, what must be the state of things in the dry? Surely it is night.

Reader, it is useless to deny these things. Humbling as it may be to the pride of human nature, the word of the Apostle is strictly true, *the time present is night*. An unconverted man may not perceive it. A graceless man may not comprehend it. The blind eye sees no difference between noon and midnight. The deaf ear makes no distinction between discord and sweet music. The mortified limb has no feeling of either heat or cold. But I do believe that God's children can enter into the meaning of the expression. The people of the Lord Jesus Christ find by experience that it is night.

It is a *cold time* to believers. They meet with much to chill and damp their zeal, and little to cheer and warm their hearts. They have to put up with many crosses and disappointments. They see iniquity abounding, and their own love is apt to become cold. And why? It is night.

It is a *lonely time* to believers. They find little company on the way that leads to heaven. Here and there they fall in with one who loves the Lord Jesus, and lives by faith. A few of God's children may be found in one town and a few in another. But on the whole the children of the world seem like the Syrian army, which filled the country, and the children of God are like a few scattered sheep in a wilderness. And why? It is night.

It is a *dangerous time* to believers. They often stumble and scarcely discern their path. They often stand in doubt, and know not which way to turn. They sometimes see not their tokens, and lose sight of their landmarks. At best they travel on in continual fear of enemies. And why? It is night.

Reader, I ask you to ponder these things. If time present be night, you will not wonder if we ministers warn Christians to watch and pray. You will count it no strange thing if we tell you to live like soldiers in an enemy's country, and to be always on your guard.

Reader, sit down and ask yourself whether you find this world in which you live to be night or day. Is time present a time of conflict or a time of ease? Do you feel that your best things are here in this life, or that your best things are yet to come? I offer these questions to you as a test of your spiritual state. I place them before you as a gauge and measure of your soul's condition. I tell you plainly, if you never found this world a wilderness and place of darkness, it is an evil sign of your state in the sight of God. The true believer will find the words of his crucified Lord to be strictly true, 'In the world ye shall have tribulation' (John 16:33). The true believer, like his Lord and Master, will be made 'perfect through sufferings'. The true believer will mourn over the world he lives in, as a world in rebellion against its rightful King. Sin will grieve him. Ungodliness will make him heavy of heart. Like Lot in Sodom, his righteous soul will be daily vexed with much that he sees and hears. He will long for the time when the day shall dawn, and the shadows flee away. For the present he will feel it is night.

Reader, is it your night or day?

2. Let us consider, in the second place, the condition of the world which is yet to come.

The Apostle Paul calls it 'day'. 'The day is at hand.'

The time here spoken of is the time to which every true Christian ought to look forward, it is the time when the Lord Jesus Christ shall come again. The present state of things in the Church of Christ shall undergo a mighty change, a change so great that it shall be like the turning of night into day.

The world we live in is not to go on always as it does now. The darkness of sin, ignorance and superstition is not always to cover the earth. The Sun of righteousness shall one day rise with healing in His wings. The Lord Jesus shall come again with power and great glory. He shall return as a morning without clouds, and then it shall be 'day'.

There is a time coming when the devil shall be bound, and shall no longer rule in this world (Rev. 20:1). Sin and all its consequences shall be cast out. The groaning creation shall at length be refreshed (Acts 3:19). The wicked shall be shut up for ever in their own place. The saints of the Most High shall at length possess the kingdom. There shall be a new heaven and a new earth, wherein shall dwell righteousness. Surely that will be 'day'.

There is a time coming when believers shall have joy and gladness, and sorrow and sighing shall flee far away. Every tear shall be wiped, every cross laid down, every anxiety removed, every bitter cup taken away. Persecution, temptation, sickness, mourning, parting, separation and death shall be at an end. Surely that will be sunshine. It will be 'day'.

There is a time coming when the whole family of Christ shall be gathered together. They shall rise from their narrow beds, and each put on a glorious body. They shall awake from their long sleep refreshed, strengthened and far more beautiful than when they lay down. They shall leave behind them in their graves every imperfection, and meet without spot or wrinkle, to part no more. Surely that will be a joyful morning. It will be 'day'.

There is a time coming when believers shall no longer see through a glass darkly, but face to face. They shall see as they have been seen, and know as they have been known. They shall cease to wrangle and dispute about outward matters, and shall think of nothing but eternal realities. They shall behold their crucified Lord and Saviour with the eye of sense, and no longer follow Him by faith. They shall see one another free from all corruption, and misunderstand one another's motives and conduct no more. Surely that will be 'day'.

I see here great comfort for every believer in Christ who reads these pages. *There is a day before you, a glorious day.* You sometimes feel now as if you walked in darkness and had no light. You have often a hard battle to fight with the world, the flesh and the devil. You sometimes fancy you will never win your way home, and must faint by the way. Your flesh and heart are ready to fail. You are sorely tempted to give up, and to sit down in despair. But take comfort in the thought of things yet to come. There is a good time before you. Your day has yet to dawn.

I see here great reason why many professing Christians should tremble and be afraid. There are many, too many I fear, to whom the time to come will be anything but day. There are many whose happiness is evidently all below, whose treasure is all on earth, whose brightest time is now and whose gloomiest prospects are hereafter. The further they look on, the darker everything appears. Old age looks dark, sickness looks darker still, death and judgment look darkest of all!

Beloved reader, if this be your case, I warn you plainly there must be a change. Your views, your tastes, your inclinations, your affections must be renewed and transformed. You must learn to view the world that now is, and that which is to come, in a very different light. Go and sit at the feet of Jesus, and ask Him to teach you this lesson. Ask for the enlightening Spirit to anoint your eyes that you may see. Ask for the veil to be taken away that you may behold everything in its true colours.

I know well that Satan labours hard to prevent men thinking of a better world than that in which we now live. He strives to turn away their eyes from the coming day. He would fain persuade them that it is impossible to do their duty in this life, and at the same time to set their affections on things above. He whispers to people that we ministers want them to become gloomy hermits, or fanatical misanthropes, and that if they listen to us they will become unfitted for all the relations of life. Against all suggestions of Satan I warn every reader to be on his guard.

I bid no one neglect the duties of his station, or forsake the post which God has called him to fill. I encourage no one in moroseness and churlishness, as if there was nothing to be thankful for in this world. I praise no one who refuses his affections to those with whom he is united by love, friendship and relationship. I only ask that the believer in the New Testament should live by a New Testament standard; that he should look for the coming day of God, and wait for the Son of God from heaven, and love his Lord's appearing.

Reader, I abhor all extravagance and fanaticism on the subject of things to come. I have no opinion of any religion which makes a man neglect his business, or cease to love his wife, children, relatives and friends. I only ask that we should take scriptural views of things as they are, and things as they yet will be. I ask that we should see our present evils and mourn over them, that we should see our future good things and long for them. Let us honestly confess that sin is around us, and long to be delivered from its presence. Let us honestly confess that holiness is one day to spread over the earth, and long for it to come. Let us never be ashamed to allow that it is 'night' and that we want it to be 'day'.

Tell me, can that man really hate sin who does not desire to see it swept away from the earth? Can that man love holiness who does not long for the time when all shall know the Lord? Can that man be truly united to Christ by faith who does not wish to see Christ, and to be with Him? Can that man be a saint who does not thirst after the unmixed company of just men made perfect? Can that man be in earnest who daily prays, 'Thy kingdom come', and yet is content that the world should go on as it is without any change? Oh, no, no! These things are impossible. God's true children will want to be at home. They will wish for the day.

Reader, if you mean to be saved, you must learn to view time present as 'night' and time to come as 'day'. You must learn to regard the other side of the Jordan as the home of your soul, and this side as a desert land. Time present must be your wilderness, your battlefield, your place of trial; time to come must be your Canaan, your rest, you Father's house, or else you had better never have been born.

3.In the third place, let us consider the particular times in which our lot is cast.

The Apostle Paul tells us, when he says, 'The night is far spent, and the day is at hand'.

I believe these words mean that the last order of things has arrived, the last stage in the history of the church has come. The law and the prophets have done their work. The Messiah promised at the fall has appeared, and provided a complete salvation. The last revelation of God's will has been made. The way of life has been laid open to all mankind. No further message from heaven to earth is to be expected before the end. No more books of Scripture are to be written. We have reached the last watch of the night. We have nothing to expect now but the sunrise and the morning.

Reader, these words, which were true eighteen hundred years ago, are, if possible, more true at the present time. They are words which should come home with increasing power to the Church of Christ every year. 'The night is far spent: the day is at hand.'

I am one of those who think 'the day' may not be so far off as some seem to suppose. I am unable to put away the idea of the Lord's return in glory as an event which 'of course' cannot be in our times, as some men say. I rather think I see tokens of the sun being near the horizon. At all events, I desire to keep in special remembrance St. James' words, 'The Judge standeth before the door, the coming of the Lord draweth nigh' and St. Peter's words 'The end of all things is at hand' (James 5:8, 9; 1 Peter 4:7).

I am no prophet and may easily be mistaken. I may die, and you may die, before Christ comes, and the day dawns. But I appeal to every thinking man whether there are not 'signs of the times' which deserve serious attention. I ask him to notice the things going in the world, and to consider well what they are intended to teach.

Does any reader ask what I mean by 'signs of the times'? Let him weigh well the six following points, and he will see what I mean.

i. What shall we say to the missions to the *heathen which* have been set on foot in these latter days? Seventy years ago the Protestant churches seemed thoroughly asleep on the subject of missions. There was hardly a single missionary sent forth to the heathen from the whole of Great Britain. The idea of preaching the gospel to savages and idolaters was ridiculed. The first promoters of missions were treated coldly by many who ought to have known better. But now the feeling is completely changed. We are employing hundreds of missionaries in every quarter of the globe. And what saith the Scripture 'The Gospel of the kingdom shall be preached in all the world for a witness unto all nations; and then shall the end come' (Matt. 24:14).

ii. What shall we say to the surprising *interest taken in the Jewish nation* in these latter days? Seventy years ago to be a Jew was a taunt, and a byword, and a proverb. No man cared for the souls of the children of Abraham. They were a people despised, and scorned, and trampled under foot. It might truly have been said, 'This is Zion, whom no man seeketh after' (Jer. 30:17). But now the feeling is completely changed. The spiritual interests of Jews are a subject of deep concern to true Christians. The civil rights of Jews are cared for even to an extreme. The very city of Jerusalem has weight in the councils of kings. Yet what saith Scripture? 'Thou shalt arise and have mercy on Zion, for the time to favour her, yea, the set time has come. For Thy servants take pleasure in her stones, and favour the dust thereof. So the heathen shall fear the name of the Lord, and all the kings of the earth Thy glory. When the Lord shall build up Zion, He shall appear in His glory' (Ps. 102:13-16).

iii. What shall we say to the wonderful *spread of knowledge and communication between nations* in these days? Seventy years ago to find a poor man who could read was rather an uncommon thing. In a few years a man who cannot read will be a rare sight. Seventy years ago there were few who ever travelled beyond the bounds of their own county. Now every one can move in every direction and our population is like a swarm of bees disturbed. Steam navigation and railways have altered the character of society. Time and space are made nothing of. Seas, mountains and rivers are no longer obstacles. God separated the nations in the day of Babel. Man is working hard to make them all one again. And what saith the Scripture? 'Shut up the words and seal the book, even to the time of the end: many shall run to and fro, and knowledge shall be increased' (Dan. 12:4).

iv. What shall we say to the wars and *shakings of nations* which we have seen in these last seventy years? The mightiest empires on earth have been shaken to their very foundations. Kings and princes and great men have been driven from their high position by scores, and been made wanderers on the face of the earth. There has been no accounting for it by any human reasoning. These movements have taken place in the face of increased knowledge, civilisation and desire of peace. The shock came from beneath. And what saith the Scripture? 'Nation shall rise against nation, and kingdom against kingdom: and there shall be famines and pestilences and earthquakes in diverse places. All these are the beginnings of sorrows' (Matt. 24: 7, 8).

v. What shall we say to the *drying up of the Mohammedan power?* Two hundred and fifty years ago, men doubted whether the Turks might not overrun all Europe! No army seemed able to resist them. Province after province fell into their hands. When Martin Luther in his sermons wanted an illustration of boundless worldly power, he would choose for his example 'the Turkish empire'! But no wall is changed. Without much outward violence the Mohammedan strength has gradually dwindled away. There has been a collapse, a consumption, a worm at the heart of all their might. In spite of all the help of the Christian allies, the Turkish empire is like a man sick of a sore disease. He may rally for a time by the help of strong remedies, and by the admission of new elements into his constitution, but he will never again be an exclusive, persecuting, purely Mohammedan power. The days of pure, intolerant Mohammedanism seem past and gone forever. And what saith the Scripture? I quote symbolical prophecy with reverence, and readily allow I may be wrong in its application; but the passage I refer to is very remarkable:

> The sixth angel poured out his vial on the great river Euphrates; and the waters thereof were dried up, that the way of the kings of the East might be prepared. And I saw three unclean spirits like frogs come out of the mouth of the dragon, and out of the mouth of the beast, and out of the mouth of the false prophet. For they are the spirits of devils, working miracles, which go forth unto the kings of the earth and of the whole world, to gather them to the battle of that great day of God Almighty. Behold I come as a thief. Blessed is he that watcheth and keepeth his garments, lest he walk naked, and they see his shame (Rev. 16:12-15).

vi. What shall we say to the *increased attention to unfulfilled prophecy*, which has appeared in these latter days? Seventy years ago there were few who paid any attention to the subject. The passages in Scripture which speak of things to come were comparatively neglected, or perverted with curious ingenuity from their simple meaning. Now, on the contrary, the current of public feeling runs strongly in favour of prophetical study. Books on the subject are eagerly bought up. Lectures on the subject are listened to with increased attention. In spite of the divisions which preterism and futurism[4] have created, in spite of the discredit which Millerites in America, and Irvingites in England, have brought upon the whole subject, the study of unfulfilled prophecy still holds its ground. But what saith the Scripture? 'The words are closed up and sealed till the time of the end' (Dan. 12:9). The words seem unfolding. The seal seems breaking. Can the end be far off?

Reader, I place these points before you, and ask your serious attention to them. I know we are all poor judges of our own times. We are apt to exaggerate the importance of events that take place under our own eyes. I dare say if we had lived in Cromwell's days, or under the first French Revolution, we should have thought the end of all things was close at hand. But still, after every allowance, I think the points I have mentioned deserve solemn consideration. I regard them as signs of our times.

I am far from saying that thee may not be wonderful changes yet before the end. I think it possible there may be a time of trouble and conflict yet 'such as never was since there was a nation' (Dan. 12:1). I believe there may yet be tribulation for the people of God 'such as was not since the beginning of the world' (Matt. 24:21). But come what will, I see a deep meaning in the words 'the night is far spent, and the day is at hand'.

I see in these words the *strongest motive for diligence* in the work of doing good to souls. Let us make more haste to spread the gospel over the world. Let us take more pains in endeavouring to sow truth at home. Let us labour, if possible, to pluck more brands from the burning. The time is short. The night is far spent. The day is at hand.

I see in these words the *strongest consolation* for the believer in Christ Jesus. Oh, for the heart to lay hold on it more and more!

Yet a little while, and believers shall part forever with *disease*. The sick and wearied ones, who have mourned over their seeming uselessness to the Church; the weak and infirm, who have had the will to labour, but not the power; the feeble and bedridden, who have waited long-drawn years in quiet chambers, till their eyes know every crack and speck on their walls; all, all shall be set free. They shall each have a glorious body like their Lord's.

Yet a little while, and mourning believers shall part forever with their *tears*. Every wound in their hearts shall be completely healed. Every empty place and gap in their affections shall be entirely filled up. They shall find that those who have died in the Lord were not lost, but gone before. They shall see that infinite wisdom arranged every bereavement, by which one was taken and another left. They shall magnify the Lord together with those who were once their companions in tribulation, and acknowledge that He did all things well, and led them by a right way.

Yet a little while, and believers shall no more feel that they are *alone*. They shall no longer be scattered over the earth, a few in one place, and a few in another. They shall no longer lament that they see so few to speak to, as a man speaketh with his friend, so few who are of one mind, and travel with them in the one narrow way. They shall be united to the general assembly and Church of the firstborn. They shall join the blessed company of all the believers of every name, and people, and tongue. Their eyes shall at length be satisfied with seeing. They shall see a multitude of saints that none can number, and not one wicked person among them.

Yet a little while, and working believers shall find that their *labour was not in vain*. The ministers who have preached and seemed to reap no fruit; the missionaries who testified of the gospel, and none seemed to believe; the teachers who poured into children's minds line upon line, and none seemed to attend; all, all shall discover that they have not spent their strength for nought. They shall find that the seed sown can spring up after many days, and that sooner or later in all labour there is profit.

Ah, reader! when shall these things be? Truly we may say, 'Lord God, Thou knowest.' A thousand years in His sight are as one day, and one day as a thousand years. But we do know that yet a little while He that shall come will come, and will not tarry. Yet a little while, and the last sermon will be preached, the last congregation shall break up. Yet a little while, and carelessness, and infidelity shall cease, perish and pass away. The believers among us will be with Christ, and the unbelievers will be in hell. The night is far spent, and the day is at hand.

4. And now, in the last place, let me speak of the particular duty of all believers, connected with the truths we have just considered.

That practical duty is put before us in plain words, 'Let us therefore cast off the works of darkness, and let us put on the armour of light.'

Reader, the word 'therefore' is often used by the Apostle Paul in a very striking and forcible way. Take a few examples, and you will at once see what I mean.

When he finishes the doctrinal part of the Epistle to the Romans, and begins his practical exhortations, what is his language? 'I beseech you *therefore* by the mercies of God, that ye present your bodies a living sacrifice, holy, acceptable to God' (Rom. 12:1).

When he has preached the resurrection of the body to the Corinthians, how does he wind up his argument? '*Therefore* my beloved brethren, be ye steadfast, unmovable' (1 Cor. 15:58).

When he has laid a mighty foundation of doctrine for the Ephesian Church, how does he proceed to address them on practical duties? 'I *therefore*, the prisoner of the Lord, beseech you that ye walk worthy of the vocation wherewith ye are called' (Eph. 4:1).

And here, as in other places, the word 'therefore' comes in upon us in a very searching and forcible way. 'The night is far spent, and the day is at hand: let us *therefore* cast off the works of darkness.'

Reader, I love to observe how closely the doctrine of Christ's second coming and kingdom is bound up with personal holiness. I marvel that any can regard the second advent and reign of the Lord Jesus as merely speculative matters, or denounce them as unprofitable subjects. To my own mind they seem eminently practical, or else I have read my Bible to very little purpose.

Does not the Apostle Paul say to the Philippians, 'Let you moderation be known unto all men: the Lord is at hand' (Phil. 4:5)?

Does he not say to the Colossians, 'Set your affections on things above, not on things on the earth. For ye are dead, and your life is hid with Christ in God. When Christ who is our life shall appear then shall ye also appear with Him in glory. Mortify therefore your members which are upon the earth' (Col. 3: 2-5)?

Does not he bid the Hebrews to 'exhort one another, and so much the more as ye see the day approaching' (Heb. 10:25)?

Does not St. Peter say, 'We look for new heavens and a new earth, wherein dwelleth righteousness. Wherefore beloved seeing that ye look for such things, be diligent that ye may be found of Him in peace without spot and blameless' (2 Peter 3: 13, 14)?

These texts appear to me to speak with no uncertain voice. I know not how their force can be evaded. They make the coming of Christ, and the day of glory, an argument for increased holiness. And it is just in the same way that St. Paul says, 'Let us cast off the works of darkness, and let us put on the armour of light'.

Reader, how are to 'cast off the works of darkness'? Listen to me and I will tell you.

You ought to lay aside everything in your life and habits which will not bear the light of Christ's appearing. You ought to make it a principle of conscience to do nothing you would not like to be found doing when Jesus comes again to gather His people together.

This is a searching test indeed. The application of it must be left to every man's own heart. Each must judge for himself. Each must prove his own works. Each must judge for himself. Each must prove his own works. Each must set up an assize within him, and honestly bring his ways to a trial. Oh, for a will to deal fairly and justly with ourselves! Oh, for a daily readiness to judge ourselves that we be not judged of the Lord, and to condemn ourselves that we be not condemned at the last day!

I ask of every reader of this address to bring the light of the day of Christ to bear upon his inner man. Set your years, and months, and weeks, and days, and hours in the full blaze of that day, and whatever thing you find within which is akin to 'darkness', pluck it out and cast it away. Keep up no questionable habit. Make no compromise with doubtful practices. Break down every idol, whether great or small. Cut down every grove, and cleanse out every chamber of imagery. Cling to nothing which would cost you a blush under the eye of Christ. Away with it at once, lest He come suddenly and put you to shame! Oh, that He may never say of any reader's heart in that day, 'This heart professed to be a temple of the Holy Ghost, but thou hast made it a den of thieves'!

Reader, try all your employment of time by the test of Christ's second coming. Place in this balance your amusements, your books, your companions, your manner of conversation, your daily behaviour in all the relations of life. Measure all by this measure, 'The night is far spent and the day is at hand. Am I living as a child of the night, or as one who looks for the day?' Do this, and you will cast off the works of darkness.

But how are you to put on the armour of light? Listen to me once more, and I will tell you.

You ought to aim at every grace and habit which becomes a believer in Christ, and a child of God, and a citizen of a heavenly kingdom. You ought not to leave eminent holiness and spirituality to a few, as if none but a few favoured ones could be eminent saints. You ought to labour to wear the armour of light yourself, the girdle of truth, the breastplate of righteousness, the helmet of hope and the sword of the Spirit (Eph. 6:14-17). Wherever you may live, and whatever may be your trials, however great your difficulties, and however small your helps, nothing should prevent your aiming at the highest standard, to behave like one who believes that Christ is coming again.

You should resolve, by God's help, so to live, that the day of Christ shall find you needing as little change as possible. You should seek to have tastes so heavenly, affections so spiritual, a will so subdued, a mind so unworldly, that when the Lord appears you may be thoroughly in tune for His kingdom. Verily it was a fine saying of Dr. Preston, on his deathbed: 'I go to change my place, but not my company.'

Ah, reader, I fear that some believers will be far less ready for the day of Christ than others. I suspect that some will have a far more abundant entrance into heaven than their brethren, more boldness, more confidence, more felt readiness for the company of their Lord. Oh, that every one into whose hands this address may fall, may so walk with God, that like Enoch, he may be only translated from a lower degree of communion to a higher! From walking by faith to walking by sight. This would be putting on the armour of light.

Let there be light in your heart continually; Christ dwelling there by faith, felt, known and experienced by your soul. Let there be light in your life continually; Christ reflected there, followed, imitated and copied. Seek to be a light in the world, and nothing less, a bright light, a clear light, a light that men can see afar off. Do this and you will put on the armour of light.

Live as if you thought Christ might come at any time. Do everything as if you did it for the last time. Say everything as if you said it for the last time. Read every chapter in the Bible as if you did not know whether you would be allowed to read it again. Pray every prayer as if you felt it might be your last opportunity. Hear every sermon as if you were hearing once and for ever. This is the way to be found ready. This is the way to turn Christ's second appearing to good account. This is the way to put on the armour of light.

1. And now perhaps this address has fallen into the hands of some *careless, thoughtless, unconverted person*. Reader, are you that man? Then remember these words, 'The night is far spent; and the day is at hand'.

What are you doing? You eat, you drink, you sleep, you dress, you work, you buy, you sell, you laugh, you read, but you do nothing for your soul. Hell is opening its mouth for you, and you are careless. Christ is coming to judge the world, and you are unprepared. Time hurries on, and you are not ready for eternity. Oh, awake to a sense of your danger and repent this day! Awake and call upon your God, before it is too late to pray. Awake and seek the Lord Jesus Christ, before the door is shut, and day of wrath begins. Alas, you may be thought wise and clever in this world, but living as you do you act the part of a madman.

2. But perhaps this address has fallen into the hands of one who is *undecided and halting between two opinions*. Reader, are you that man? Then remember these words 'The night is far spent, and the day is at hand'.

What are you doing? You hear, you listen, you wish, you desire, you mean, you intend, you hope, you resolve, but you go no further. You see the ark, but you will not go in. You see the bread of life, but you do not eat it. You wait. And yet time gets on. The devil is saying over you, 'I shall have this soul before long.' Oh, come out from the world and linger no more! Take up the cross. Cast away vain excuses. Confess Christ before men. Beware, I say, lest you make up your mind too late. Again I say, beware.

3. But perhaps this address has fallen into the hands of some *true believer*. Reader, are you that man? Then remember these words. 'The night is far spent, and the day is at hand.'

I ask you to live as if you believed the words we have been considering, and to show the world you think them true. The nearer you draw to home, the more wakeful you ought to be. The more you realise the second personal coming of the Lord Jesus, the more lively ought your Christianity to be.

Ah, reader, it is but too true, as Leigh Richmond said on his deathbed, 'We are but half awake! We are but half awake!' The best of us need to have our hearts stirred up by way of remembrance. Let us rub the sleepy eyes of our mind, and look the speedy coming of our Master full in the face. Let the time past suffice us to have been drowsy and lazy servants. For the time to come let us work like those who feel, 'The Master will soon be here.'

I remember, when I was a schoolboy, I could wake up, however tired with a long journey, when I began to draw near home. Soon as I saw the old hills, and trees, and chimneys, the sense of weariness was gone, and I was all alive. The prospect of soon seeing much-loved faces, the joy of thinking of a family gathering, all this was able to drive sleep away. Surely it ought to be the same with us in the matter of our souls. The night is far spent, and the day is at hand. Yet a little while, and He that shall come will come and will not tarry. Then let us cast off every work of darkness. Let us put on the whole armour of light. Let us be ashamed of our past drowsiness. Let us awake, and sleep no more.

Romans 13:12

Soon and for ever, the breaking of day
Shall chase all the night-clouds of sorrow away;
Soon, and for ever, we'll see as we're seen,
And know the deep meaning of things that have been,
Where fightings without and conflicts within
Shall weary no more in the warfare with sin,
Where tears and where fears and where death shall be never,
Christians with Christ shall be soon, and for ever!

Soon, and for ever, such promise our trust,
Though ashes to ashes, and dust to dust,
Soon, and for ever, our union shall be
Made perfect, our glorious Redeemer in Thee;
When the cares and the sorrows of time shall be o'er,
Its pangs and its partings remembered no more,

Where life cannot fail and where death cannot sever,
Christians with Christ shall be soon and for ever!

Soon, and for ever, the work shall be done,
The warfare accomplished, the victory won;
Soon, and for ever, the soldier lay down
The sword for a harp, the cross for a crown;
Then droop not in sorrow, despond not in fear,
A glorious tomorrow is bright'ning and near,
When, blessed reward for each faithful endeavour,
Christians with Christ shall be soon, and for ever!

Monsell

2 Timothy 4:8

Come, Lord, and tarry not:
Bring the long-looked-for day;
Oh, why these years of waiting here,
These ages of delay?

Come, for Thy saints still wait;
Daily ascends their sigh;
The Spirit and the bride say,
Come, dost Thou not hear the cry?

Come, for Thy Israel pines,
An exile from My fold;
Oh, all to mind Thy faithful word,
And bless them as of old!

Come, for the good are few;
They lift their voice in vain;
Faith waxes fainter on the earth,
And love is on the wane.

Come, for the corn is ripe;
Put in Thy sickle now,
Reap the great harvest of the earth,
Sower and Reaper Thou!

Come, in Thy glorious might,
Come, with the iron rod,
Scattering Thy foes before
Thy face, Most Mighty Son of God.

Come, and make all things new,
Build up this ruined earth,
Restore our faded Paradise,
Creation's second birth.

Come, and begin Thy reign
Of everlasting peace;
Come, take the kingdom to Thyself,
Great King of righteousness.

H Bonar

4

IDOLATRY TO BE DESTROYED
AT CHRIST'S COMING

The idols He shall utterly abolish (Isa. 2:18)

The time here spoken of will be plain to all who take the prophecy of Isaiah in its literal meaning. It is the second coming of our Lord Jesus Christ, the day when 'He ariseth to shake terribly the earth'. The event is part of that mighty purification which will then take place in His professing Church, the abolishing of all idols; and the principal subject which claims your consideration in the text is idolatry.

Without further preface, I desire to ask your attention to the four following points:

1. *The definition of idolatry*. WHAT IS IT?
2. *The cause of idolatry*. WHENCE COMES IT?
3. *The form of idolatry assumes in the visible Church of Christ*. WHERE IS IT?
4. *The ultimate abolition of idolatry*. WHAT WILL END IT?

I feel that the subject is encompassed with many difficulties. Our lot is cast in an age when truth is constantly in danger of being sacrificed to toleration, charity and peace falsely so called. Nevertheless, I cannot forget that I am a minister of a Church which has given no uncertain sound on the subject of idolatry; and, unless I am greatly mistaken, truth about idolatry is, in the highest sense, truth for the times.

1. Let me, then, first of all set before you the *definition of idolatry*. Let me show you WHAT IT IS.

It is of the utmost importance that you should understand this. Unless I make this clear, I can do nothing with the text. Vagueness and indistinctness prevail upon this point, as upon almost every other in religion. The Christian that would not be continually running aground in his spiritual voyage, must have his channel well buoyed, his mind well stored with clear definitions.

I say then, that *idolatry is a worship, in which the honour due to God in Trinity, and to Him only, is given to some of His creatures, or some invention of His creatures.* It may vary exceedingly. It may assume exceedingly different forms, according to the ignorance or the knowledge, the civilisation or the barbarism, of those who offer it. It may be grossly absurd and ludicrous, or it may closely border on truth, and admit of being most speciously defended. But whether in the adoration of the idol of Juggernaut, or in the adoration of the host in St. Peter's at Rome, the idolatrous principle is in reality the same. In either case the honour due to God is turned aside from Him, and bestowed on that which is not God. And whenever this is done, whether in heathen temples or in professedly Christian churches, there is an act of idolatry.

You must bear in mind that it is not necessary for a man formally to deny God and Christ in order to be an idolater. Far from it. Professed reverence for the God of the Bible and actual idolatry are perfectly compatible. They have often gone side by side, and they still do so. The children of Israel never thought of renouncing God when they persuaded Aaron to make the golden calf. 'These by thy gods,' they said (thy Elohim), 'which brought thee up out of the land of Egypt.' And the feast in honour of the calf was kept as 'a feast unto the Lord' (Jehovah) (Exod. 32:4, 5). Jeroboam, again, never pretended to ask the ten tribes to cast off their allegiance to the God of David and Solomon. When he set up the calves of gold in Dan and Bethel, he only said, 'It is too much for you to go up to Jerusalem: behold thy gods, O Israel (thy Elohim), which brought thee up out of the land of Egypt' (1 Kings 12:28). In both instances, you will observe the idol was not set up as a rival to God, but under the pretence of being a help, a stepping-stone to His service. But, in both instances, you know well, a great sin was committed. The honour due to God was given to a visible representation of Him. The majesty of Jehovah was offended. The second commandment was broken. There was, in the eyes of God, a flagrant act of idolatry.

I ask you to mark this, my brethren. I ask you to dismiss from your minds those loose ideas about idolatry, which are common in this day. Think not, as many do, that there are only two sorts of idolatry, the spiritual idolatry of the man who loves his wife or child or money more than God, and the open, gross idolatry of the man who bows down to an image of wood, or metal, or stone, because he knows no better. Depend upon it, idolatry is a sin that occupies a far, far wider field than this. It is not merely a thing in Hindostan, that you may hear of and pit at missionary meetings; nor yet is it a thing confined to your own heart, that you may confess before the mercyseat upon your knees. It is a pestilence that walks in the Church of Christ to a much greater extent than many of you suppose. It is an evil that, like the man of sin, 'sits in the very temple of God' (2 Thess. 2:4). It is a sin that we all need to watch and pray against continually. It creeps into our religious worship insensibly, and is upon us before we are aware. Those are tremendous words which Isaiah spoke to the formal Jew, not to the worshipper of Baal, remember, but to the man who actually came to the temple (Isa. 66:3): 'He that killeth an ox is as if he slew a man; he that sacrificeth a lamb, as if he cut off a dog's neck; he that offereth an oblation as if he offered swine's blood; he that burneth incense as if he blessed an idol.'

This is that sin, remember, which God has specially denounced in His Word. One commandment out of ten is devoted to the prohibition of it. None of all the ten contain such a solemn declaration of His character and of His judgments against the disobedient: 'I the Lord thy God am a jealous God, visiting the iniquity of the fathers upon the children unto the third and fourth generation of them that hate Me' (Exod. 20:5). None, perhaps, of all the ten is so emphatically repeated and amplified, and especially in the fourth chapter of the book of Deuteronomy.

This is the sin of all others which has brought down the heaviest judgments on the visible Church. It brought on Israel the armies of Egypt, Assyria and Babylon. It scattered the ten tribes, burned up Jerusalem, and carried Judah and Benjamin into captivity. It brought on the Eastern churches, in later days, the overwhelming flood of the Saracenic invasion, and turned many a spiritual garden into a wilderness. The desolation which reigns where Cyprian and Augustine once preached, the living death in which the churches of Asia Minor and Syria are buried, are all attributable to this sin. All testify to the same great truth which the Lord proclaims in Isaiah, 'My glory will I not give to another' (Isa. 42:8).

Gather up these things in your mind, beloved brethren. Be very sure that idolatry is a subject which in every Church of Christ that would keep herself pure, should be thoroughly examined, understood and known.

2.Let me show you, in the second place, the cause to which idolatry may be traced. WHENCE COMES IT?

To the man who takes an extravagant and exalted view of human intellect and reason, idolatry may seem absurd. He fancies it too irrational for any but weak minds to be endangered by it.

To a mere superficial thinker about Christianity, the peril of idolatry may seem very small. Whatever commandments are broken, such a man will tell us, professing Christians are not very likely to transgress the second.

Now, both these persons betray a woeful ignorance of human nature. They do not see that there are secret roots of idolatry within us all. The prevalence of idolatry in all ages among the heathen must necessarily puzzle the one, the warnings of Protestant ministers against the idolatry in the Church must necessarily appear uncalled for to the other, since both are alike blind to its cause.

The cause of all idolatry is the natural corruption of man's heart. That great family disease, with which all the children of Adam are born, shows itself in this, as it does in a thousand other ways. Out of the same fountain from which 'proceed evil thoughts, adulteries, fornications, murders, thefts, covetousness, wickedness, deceit' and the like (Mark 7: 21, 22), out of that same fountain arise false views of God, and false views of the worship due to Him; and, therefore, when the Apostle Paul tells the Galatians (Gal. 5:20) what are the 'works of the flesh' he places prominently among them 'idolatry'.

A religion of some kind, man will have. God has not left Himself without a witness in us all, fallen as we are. Like old inscriptions hidden under mounds of rubbish, like the almost obliterated underwriting of Palimpsest manuscripts, even so there is a dim *something* engraven at the bottom of man's heart, however faint and half-erased, a *something* which makes him feel he must have a religion and a worship of some kind. The proof of this is to be found in the history of voyages and travels in every part of the globe. The exceptions to the rule are so few, if, indeed, there are any, that they only confirm its truth. Man's worship in some dark corner of the earth may rise no higher than a vague fear of an evil spirit and a desire to propitiate him, but a worship of some kind, man will have.

But then comes in the effect of the fall. Ignorance of God, carnal and low conceptions of His nature and attributes, earthly and sensual notions of the service which is acceptable to Him, all characterise the religion of the natural man. There is a craving in his mind after something he can see, and feel, and touch in his divinity. He would fain bring his God down to his own crawling level. He would make his religion a thing of sense and sight. He has no idea of faith and spirit. In short, just as he is willing to live on God's earth, but until renewed by grace, a fallen and degraded life, so he has no objection to worship after a fashion, but, until renewed by the Holy Ghost, it is always with a fallen worship. In one word, idolatry is a natural product of man's heart. It is a weed, which like the earth uncultivated, the heart is always ready to bring forth.

And now does it surprise you, when you read of the constantly recurring idolatries of the Old Testament Church, of Peor, and Baal, and Moloch, and Chemosh, and Ashtoreth, of high places and hill altars, and groves and images, and this in the full light of the Mosaic ceremonial? Cease to be surprised. It can be accounted for. There is a cause.

Does it surprise you, when you read in history, how idolatry crept in by degrees into the Church of Christ, how little by little it thrust out gospel truth, until, in Canterbury, men offered more at the shrine of Thomas à Becket, than they did at that of the Virgin Mary, and more at that of the Virgin Mary, than at that of Christ? Cease to be surprised. It is all intelligible. There is a cause.

Does it surprise you, when you hear of men going over from Protestant churches to the Church of Rome, in the present day? Do you think it unaccountable, and feel as if you yourself could never forsake a pure form of worship for one like that of the Pope? Cease to be surprised. There is a solution for the problem. There is a cause.

That cause is nothing else but the deep corruption of man's heart. There is a natural proneness and tendency in us all to give God a sensual, carnal worship, and not that which is commanded in His Word. We are ever ready to frame for our sloth and unbelief, visible helps and stepping-stones in our approaches to Him, and ultimately to give these inventions of our own the honour due to Him. In fact, idolatry is all natural, downhill, easy, like the broad way. Spiritual worship is all of grace, all uphill and all against the grain. Any worship whatsoever is more pleasing to the natural heart, than worshipping God, in the way our Lord Jesus Christ describes, 'in spirit and in truth' (John 4:23).

I, for one, am not surprised at the quantity of idolatry existing both in the world, and in the visible Church. I believe it perfectly possible that we may live to see more of it yet, than some have ever dreamed of. It would never surprise me, if some mighty personal antichrist were to arise before the end, mighty in intellect, mighty in talents for government, aye, and mighty perhaps in miraculous gifts too. It would never surprise me to see such a one as him setting up himself in opposition to Christ, and making an infidel combination against the gospel. I believe that many would rejoice to do him honour, who now glory in saying, 'We will not have this Christ to reign over us.' I believe that many would make a god of him, and reverence him as an incarnation of truth, and concentrate their idea of hero-worship on his person. I advance it as a possibility, and no more. But of this at last I am certain, that no man is less safe from danger of idolatry than the man who now sneers at every form of religion; and that from infidelity to credulity, from Atheism to the grossest idolatry, there is but a single step. Think not, at all events, beloved brethren, that idolatry is an old-fashioned sin, into which you are never likely to fall. 'Let him that thinketh he standeth take heed lest he fall.' Look into your own hearts. The seeds of idolatry are all there.

3. Let me show you, in the third place, the forms which idolatry has assumed, and does assume in the visible Church. WHERE IS IT?

I believe there never was a more baseless fabric than the theory which obtains favour with many, that the promises of perpetuity and preservation from apostasy, belong to the visible Church of Christ. It is a theory supported neither by Scripture, nor by facts. The Church against which the gates of hell shall never prevail, is not the visible Church, but the whole body of the elect, the company of true believers out of every nation and people. The greater part of the visible Church has frequently maintained gross heresies. The particular branches of it are never secure against deadly error, both of faith and practice. A departure from the faith, a falling away, a leaving of first love in any branch of the visible Church, need never surprise a careful reader of the New Testament.

That idolatry would arise, seems to have been the expectation of the Apostles, even before the canon of the New Testament was closed. It is remarkable to observe how St. Paul dwells on this subject in his Epistle to the Corinthians. If any Corinthian, called a brother, was an idolater, with such a one the members of the church were not to eat (1 Cor. 5:11). 'Neither be ye idolaters, as were some of our fathers' (1 Cor. 10:7). He says again, 'My dearly beloved, flee from idolatry' (1 Cor. 10: 14). When he writes to the Colossians, he warns them against 'worshipping of angels' (Col. 2:18). And St. John closes his first Epistle with the solemn injunction, 'Little children, keep yourselves from idols' (1 John 5:21). It is impossible not to feel that all these passages imply an expectation that idolatry would arise, and that soon, among professing Christians.

The famous prophecy in the fourth chapter of the first Epistle to Timothy contains a passage which is ever more directly to the point: 'The Spirit speaketh expressly, that in the latter times some shall depart from the faith, giving heed to seducing spirits, and doctrines of devils' (1 Tim. 4:1). I will not detain you with any lengthy discussion of that remarkable expression 'doctrines of devils'. It may be sufficient to say, that our excellent translators are considered for once to have missed the full meaning of the Apostle, in their rendering of the word translated 'devils' in our version, and that the true meaning of the expression is 'doctrines about departed spirits'. And in this view, which, I may as well say, is maintained by all those who have the best right to be heard on such a question, the passage becomes a direct prediction of the rise of that most specious form of idolatry, the *worship of dead saints.*

The last passage I will call to your attention to, is the conclusion of the ninth chapter of Revelation. We there read, at the twentieth verse: 'The rest of the men which were not killed by these plagues, yet repented not of the works of their hands, that they should not worship devils' (mark, this is the same word as that in the Epistle to Timothy, just quoted), 'and idols of gold, and silver, and brass, and stone and wood: which neither can see, nor hear, nor walk'. Now, I am not going to offer any comment on the chapter in which this verse occurs. I know well there is a difference of opinion as to the true interpretation of the plagues predicted in it. One thing I venture to assert, that it is the highest probability these plagues are to fall upon the visible church of Christ; and the highest improbability, that St. John was here prophesying about the heathen, who never heard the Gospel. And this once conceded, the fact that idolatry is a predicted sin of the visible Church, does seem most conclusively and forever established.

And now, if we turn from the Bible to facts, what do we see? I reply unhesitatingly, that there is unmistakable proof that Scripture warnings and predictions were not spoken without cause, and that idolatry has actually arisen in the visible Church of Christ, and does still exist.

The rise and progress of the evil in former days, you will find well summed up in the admirable Homily of our own Church, on Peril of Idolatry. To that Homily I beg to refer you, reminding you once for all, that in the judgment of your own thirty-nine Articles, the Book of Homilies 'contains a godly and wholesome doctrine, and necessary for these times'.

There you will read, how, even in the fourth century, Jerome complains that the errors of images have come in, and passed to the Christians from the Gentiles', and Eusebius says, 'We do see now that images of Peter and Paul, and of our Saviour Himself be made, and tables be painted, which I think to have been derived and kept indifferently by an heathenish custom.'

There you will read, how 'Pontius Paulinus, Bishop of Nola, in the *fifth century*, caused the walls of the temples to be painted with stories taken out of the Old Testament; that the people beholding and considering these pictures, might the better abstain from too much surfeiting and riot. But from learning by painted stories, it came by little and little to idolatry'.

There you will read how Gregory the First, Bishop of Rome, in the beginning of the *seventh century*, did allow the free having of images in churches.

There you will read how Irene, mother of Constantine the Sixth, in the *eighth century*, assembled a council at Nicaea, and procured a decree that 'images should be put up in all the churches of Greece and that honour and worship should be given to the said images'.

And there you will read the conclusion with which the Homily winds up its historical summary, 'that laity and clergy, learned and unlearned, all ages, sorts, and degrees of men, women and children of whole Christendom, have been at once drowned in abominable idolatry, of all other vices most detested of God, and most damnable to man, and that by the space of 800 years and more.'

This is a mournful account, beloved brethren, but it is only too true. There can be little doubt the evil began before the time just mentioned by the Homily writers, No man, I think, need wonder at the vice of idolatry in the primitive Church who considers calmly the excessive reverence which it paid, from the very first, to the visible parts of religion. I believe that no impartial man can read the language used by nearly all the Fathers about the Church, the bishops, the ministry, baptism, the Lord's Supper, the martyrs, the dead saints generally – no man can read it, without being struck with the wide difference between their language and the language of Scripture on such subjects. You seem at once to be in a new atmosphere. You feel that you are no longer treading on holy ground. You find things which, in the Bible, are evidently of second-rate importance, are here made of first-rate importance. You find the things of sense and sight exalted to a position in which Paul, and Peter, and James, and John, speaking by the Holy Ghost, never for a moment placed them.

It is not merely the weakness of uninspired writings that you have to complain of; it is something worse: it is a new system. And what is the explanation of all this? It is, in one word, that you have got into a region where the malaria of idolatry has begun to arise. You perceive the first workings of the mystery of iniquity. You detect the buds of that huge system of idolatry which, as the Homily describes, was afterwards formally acknowledged, and ultimately blossomed so luxuriantly in every part of Christendom.

But let us now turn from the past to the present. Let us examine the question which most concerns ourselves. Let us consider in what form idolatry presents itself to us as a sin of the visible Church of Christ in our own time.

I find no difficulty in answering this question. I feel no hesitation in affirming that idolatry never yet assumed a more glaring form than it does in the Church of Rome at this very day.

And here I come to a subject on which it is hard to speak, because of the times we live in. But the whole truth ought to be spoken by ministers of Christ, without respect of times and prejudice. And I should not lie down in peace, after preaching on idolatry, if I did not declare my solemn conviction, that idolatry is one of the crying sins of which the Church of Rome is guilty. I say this in all sadness. I say it, acknowledging fully that we have our faults in our own church: and practically, perhaps in some quarters, not a little idolatry. But formal, recognised, systematic idolatry, I believe we are free from at all events. While, as for the Church of Rome, if there is not in her worship an enormous quantity of systematic, organised idolatry, I frankly confess I do not know what idolatry is.

To my mind, it is idolatry to have images and pictures of saints in churches, and to give them a reverence for which there is no warrant or precedent in Scripture. And if this be so, I say there is idolatry in the Church of Rome.

To my mind, it is idolatry to invoke the Virgin Mary and the saints in glory, and to address them in language never addressed in Scripture except to the Holy Trinity. And if this be so, I say there is idolatry in the Church of Rome.

To my mind, it is idolatry to bow down to mere material things, and attribute to them a power and sanctity far exceeding that attached to the ark or altar of the Old Testament dispensation, and a power and sanctity, too, for which there is not a tittle of foundation in the Word of God. And if this be so, with the holy coat of Treves and the wonderfully multiplied wood of the true cross, and a thousand other so-called relics in my mind's eye, I say there is idolatry in the Church of Rome.

To my mind, it is idolatry to worship that which man's hands have made, to call it God, and adore it when lifted up before our eyes. And if this be so, with the doctrine of transubstantiation, and the elevation of the host in my recollect, I say there is idolatry in the Church of Rome.

To my mind, it is idolatry to make ordained men mediators between ourselves and God, robbing, as it were our Lord Jesus Christ of His office, and giving them an honour which even Apostles and angels in Scripture flatly repudiate. And if this be so, with the honour paid to popes and priests before my eyes, I say there *is idolatry in the Church of Rome.*

I know well that language like this jars the minds of many. Men love to shut their eyes against evils which it is disagreeable to allow. They will not see things which involve unpleasant consequences. That the Church of Rome is an erring church, they will acknowledge. That she *is idolatrous*, they will deny.

They tell us, that the reverence which the Romish Church gives to saints and images does not amount to idolatry. They inform us that there are distinctions between 'latria' and 'dulia', between a mediation of redemption, and a mediation of intercession, which clear her of the charge. My answer is, that the Bible knows nothing of such distinctions; and that, in the actual practice of the great bulk of Roman Catholics, they have no existence at all.

They tell us, that it is a mistake to suppose that Roman Catholics really worship the images and pictures before which they perform acts of adoration; that they only use them as helps to devotion, and in reality look far beyond them. My answer is, that many a heathen could say just as much for his idolatry: that it is notorious, in former days, they did say so, and that in Hindostan many idol worshippers do say so at the present day. But the apology does not avail. The terms of the second commandment are too stringent. It prohibits *bowing down*, as well as worshipping. And the very anxiety which the Church of Rome has often displayed to exclude that second commandment from her catechisms, is of itself a great fact which speaks volumes to a candid observer.

They tell us that we have no evidence for the assertions we make on this subject; that we found our charges on the abuses which prevail among the ignorant members of the Romish communion; and that it is absurd to say, that a Church containing so many wise and learned men, is guilty of idolatry. My answer is, that the devotional books in common use among Roman Catholics supply us with unmistakable evidence. Let any one examine that notorious book *The Garden of the Soul* if he doubts my assertion, and read the language there addressed to the Virgin Mary. Let him remember that this language is addressed to a woman, who, though highly favoured, and the mother of our Lord, was yet one of our fellow sinners, who actually confesses her need of a Saviour for herself. She says, 'My spirit hath rejoiced in God my Saviour' (Luke 1:47). Let him examine this language in the light of the New Testament, and then let him tell us fairly whether the charge of idolatry is not fully made out. But I answer, besides this, that we want no better evidence than that which is supplied in the city of Rome itself. What do men and women do under the light of the Pope's own countenance? What is the religion that prevails around St. Peter's and under the walls of the Vatican? What is Romanism at Rome, unfettered, unshackled and free to develop itself in full perfection? Let a man honestly answer these questions, and I ask no more. Let him read such a book as Seymour's *Pilgrimage to Rome* or Alford's *Letters*, and ask any visitor to Rome if the picture is too highly coloured. Let him do this, I say, and I believe he cannot avoid this conclusion, that Romanism in perfection is a gigantic system of Mary worship, saint worship, image worship, relic worship, and priest worship; that it is, in one word, a huge organised idolatry.

Brethren, I know not how these things sound to your ears. To me it is no pleasure to dwell on the shortcomings of any who profess and call themselves Christians. I can say truly, that I have said what I have said with pain and sorrow.

I draw a wide distinction between the Church of Rome; and the private opinions of many of her members. I believe and hope that many a Roman Catholic is in heart inconsistent with his profession, and is better than the church to which he belongs. I cannot forget the Jansenists, and Quesnel, and Martin Boos. I believe that many a poor Italian at this day is worshipping with an idolatrous worship simply because he knows no better. He has no Bible to instruct him. he has no faithful minister to teach him. He has the fear of the priest before his eyes if he dares to think for himself. He has no money to enable him to get away from the bondage he lives under, even if he feels a desire. I remember all this, and I say that the Italian eminently deserves our sympathy and compassion; but all this must not prevent my saying that the Church of Rome is an idolatrous church.

I should not be faithful if I said less. The church of which I am a minister has spoken out most strongly on the subject. The Homily on the Peril of Idolatry, and the solemn protest following the Rubrics, at the end of our Communion Service, which denounces the adoration of the sacramental bread and wine as 'idolatry to be abhorred of all faithful Christians', are plain evidence that I have told you no more than the mind of my own church. And in a day like this, when some are disposed to secede to the Church of Rome, and many are shutting their eyes to her real character, and wanting us to be reunited to her, in a day like this, my own conscience would rebuke me if

I did not warn men plainly that the Church of Rome is an idolatrous church, and that if they will join her they are '*joining themselves to idols*'.

But I may not dwell longer on this part of my subject. The main point I wish to impress on your minds is this, that idolatry has decidedly manifested itself in the visible Church of Christ, and nowhere so decidedly as in the Church of Rome.

4. And now let me show you, in the last place, the ultimate abolition of all idolatry. WHAT WILL END IT?

I consider that man's soul must be in an unhealthy state, who does not long for the time when idolatry shall be no more. That heart can hardly be right with God which can think of the millions who are sunk in heathenism, or honour the false prophet Mohammed, or daily invoke the Virgin Mary, and not cry, 'O my God, what shall be the end of these things? How long, O God, how long?

Here, as in other subjects, the sure word of prophecy comes in to our aid. The end of all idolatry shall one day come. Its doom is fixed. Its overthrow is certain. Whether in heathen temples, or in so-called Christian churches, idolatry shall be destroyed at the second coming of our Lord Christ.

Then shall be fulfilled the prophecy of our text: 'The idols He shall utterly abolish.' So also the prophecy of Micah 5:13: 'Their graven images also will I cut off, and their standing images out of the midst of thee, and thou shalt no more worship the work of thine hands.' So also the prophecy of Zephaniah 2:11: 'The LORD will be terrible unto them: for He will smash all the gods of the earth; and men shall worship Him, every one from his place, even all the isles of the heathen.' So also the prophecy of Zechariah 13:2: 'It shall come to pass at that day, saith the LORD of hosts, that I will cut off the names of the idols out of the land, and they shall no more be remembered.'

In a word, the 97th Psalm shall then receive its full accomplishment:

The LORD reigneth: let the earth rejoice; let the multitude of isles be glad thereof. Clouds and darkness are round about Him: righteousness and judgment are the habitation of His throne. A fire goeth before Him, and burneth up His enemies round about. His lightnings enlightened the world: the earth saw and trembled. The hills melted like wax at the presence of the LORD, at the presence of the Lord of the whole earth. The heavens declare His righteousness, and all the people see His glory. Confounded be all they that serve graven images, that boast themselves of idols: worship Him, all ye gods.

Brethren, the coming and kingdom of our Lord Jesus Christ is that blessed hope which should ever comfort the children of God under the present dispensation. It is the polestar by which we must journey. It is the one point on which all our expectations should be concentrated. 'Yet a little while, and He that shall come will come, and will not tarry.' Our David shall no longer dwell in Adullam, followed by a despised few, and rejected by the many. He shall take to Himself his great power, and reign, and cause every knee to bow before Him.

Till then our redemption is not perfectly enjoyed; as Paul tells the Ephesians, 'We are sealed unto the day of redemption' (Eph. 4:30). Our salvation is not completed; as Peter says 'We are kept by the power of God through faith unto salvation ready to be revealed in the last time' (1 Peter 1:5). Our knowledge is still defective; as Paul tells the Corinthians: 'Now we see through a glass darkly; but then face-to-face; now I know in part; then shall I know even also as I am known' (1 Cor. 13:12). In short, our best things are yet to come.

But in the day of our Lord's return every desire shall receive its full accomplishment. We shall no more be pressed down and worn out with the sense of constant failure, feebleness and disappointment. In His presence we shall find there is a *fullness* of joy, if nowhere else; and when we awake up after His likeness we shall be *satisfied*, if we never were before.

There are many abominations now in the visible Church, over which we can only sigh and cry, like the faithful in Ezekiel's day (Ezek. 9:4). We cannot remove them. But a day comes when Jesus shall once more purify His temple, and cast forth everything that defiles. He shall do that work of which the doings of Hezekiah and Josiah were a faint type long ago. He shall cast forth the images, and purge out idolatry in every shape.

Who is there among you that longs for the conversion of the heathen world? You will not see it in its fullness until the Lord's appearing. Then, and not till then, will that often misapplied text be fulfilled: 'A man shall cast his idols of silver, and his idols of gold, which they made each one for himself to worship, to the moles and to the bats' (Isa. 2:20).

Who is there among you that longs for the redemption of Israel? You will never see it in its perfection till the Redeemer come to Zion. Idolatry in the professing Church of Christ has been one of the mightiest stumbling-blocks in the Jews' way. When it begins to fall, the veil over the heart of Israel shall begin to be taken away (Ps. 102:16).

Who is there among you that longs for the fall of antichrist, and the purification of the Church of Rome? I believe that will never be until the winding up of this dispensation. That vast system of idolatry may be consumed and wasted by the spirit of the Lord's mouth, but it shall never be destroyed excepting by the brightness of His coming (2 Thess. 2:8).

Who is there among you that longs for a perfect Church, a Church in which there shall not be the slightest taint of idolatry? You must wait for the Lord's return. Then, and not till then, shall we see a perfect Church, a Church having neither spot nor wrinkle, nor any such thing (Eph. 5:27), a Church of which all the members shall be regenerate, and every one a child of God.

Brethren, if these things be so, you will not wonder that we urge on you the study of prophecy, and that we charge you above all to grasp firmly the glorious doctrine of Christ's second appearing and kingdom. This is the light shining in a dark place to which you will do well to take heed. Let others indulge their imagination if they will, with an imaginary 'Church of the future'. Let the children of this world dream of some 'coming man' who is to understand everything, and set everything right. They are only sowing to themselves bitter disappointment. They will awake to find their visions baseless and empty as a dream. It is to such as these that the Prophet's words may be well applied: 'Behold all ye that kindle a fire, that compass yourselves about with sparks: walk in the light of your fire, and in the sparks that ye have kindled. This shall ye have of Mine hand; ye shall lie down in sorrow' (Isa. 1:11).

But let your eyes look right onward to the day of Christ's second advent. That is the only day when ever abuse shall be rectified, and every corruption and source of sorrow completely purged away. Waiting for that day, let us each work on and serve our generation; not idle, as if nothing could be done to check evil, but not disheartened because we see not yet all things put under our Lord. After all, the night is far spent, and the day is at hand. Let us wait, I say, on the Lord.

And surely, if these things be so, you will not wonder that we warn you to beware of all leanings towards the Church of Rome. Surely, when the mind of God about idolatry is so plainly revealed to us in His Word, it seems the height of infatuation in any one to join a church so steeped in idolatries as the Church of Rome. To enter into communion with her, when God is saying, 'Come out of her, that ye be not partakers of her sins, and receive not of her plagues' (Rev. 18:4), to seek her when the Lord is warning us to leave her, to become her subjects when the Lord's voice is crying, 'Escape for thy life, flee from the wrath to come', all this is mental blindness indeed, a blindness like that of him who, though forewarned, embarks in a sinking ship, a blindness that would be almost incredible, if our own eyes did not see examples of it continually.

We must all be on our guard. We must take nothing for granted. We must not hastily suppose that we are too wise to be ensnared, and say, like Hazael, 'Is Thy servant a dog, that he should do this thing' We who preach must cry aloud and spare not, and allow no false tenderness to make us hold our peace about the heresies of the day. You who hear must have your loins girt about with truth, and your minds stored with clear prophetical views of the end to which all idol worshippers must come. Let us all try to realise that the latter ends of the world are upon us, and that the abolition of all idolatry is hastening on. Is this a time for a man to draw nearer to Rome? Is it not rather a time to draw further back and stand clear, lest we be involved in her downfall? Is this a time to extenuate and palliate Rome's manifold corruptions, and refuse to see the reality of her sins? Surely we ought rather to be doubly jealous of everything of a Romish tendency in religion, doubly careful that we do not connive at any treason against our Lord Jesus Christ, and doubly ready to protest against unscriptural worship of every description. Once more, then, I say, remember that the destruction of all idolatry is certain, and remembering that, beware of the Church of Rome.

And now it only remains for me to conclude what I have been saying, by mentioning some safeguards for your own souls. You live in a time when the Church of Rome is walking amongst us with renewed strength, and loudly boasting that she will soon win back the ground that she has lost. False doctrines of every kind are continually set before you in the most subtle and specious forms. It cannot be thought unseasonable if I offer you some practical safeguards against idolatry. What it is, whence it comes, where it is, what will end it, all this you have heard. Let me point out how you may be safe from it, and I will say no more.

1. Arm yourselves, then, for one thing, with a thorough knowledge of the Word of God. Read it more diligently than ever. Become familiar with every part of it. Let it dwell in you richly. Beware of anything which would make you give less time, and less heart to the perusal of its sacred pages. The Bible is the sword of the Spirit; let it never be laid aside. The Bible is the true lantern for a dark and cloudy time; beware of travelling without its light. I strongly suspect, if we did but know the secret history of those secessions, from our church to that of Rome, which we deplore, I strongly

suspect that in almost every case one of the most important steps in the downward road would be found to have been a neglected Bible – more attention to forms, sacraments, daily services, primitive Christianity, and so forth, and diminished attention to the written Word of God. The Bible is the King's highway. Once leave that for any bypath, however beautiful and old and frequented it may seem, and never be surprised if you end with worshipping images and relics.

2. Arm yourselves, in the second place, with a godly jealousy about the least portion of the gospel. Beware of sanctioning the slightest attempt to keep back any jot or tittle of it, or to throw any part of it into the shade by exalting subordinate matters in religion. It seemed a small thing that Peter did when he withdrew himself from eating with the Gentiles, but Paul tells the Galatians, 'I withstood him to the face, because he was to be blamed' (Gal. 2:11). Count nothing little that concerns your soul. Be very particular whom you hear, where you go and what you do, in all the matters of your own particular worship. Care nothing for the imputation of squeamishness and excessive scrupulosity. You live in days when great principles are involved in little acts, and things in religion, which fifty years ago were utterly indifferent, are now by circumstances rendered indifferent no longer. Beware of tampering with anything of a Romanising tendency. It is foolishness to play with fire. I believe that many of our seceders began with thinking there could be nor mighty harm attaching a *little* more importance to certain outward things than they once did. But once launched on the downward course, they went from one thing to another. They provoked God, and He left them to themselves. They tempted the devil, and he came to them. They started with trifles, as many foolishly call them. They have ended with downright idolatry.

3. Arm yourselves, last of all, and above all, with clear, sound views of our Lord Jesus Christ, and of the salvation that is in Him. He is the image of the invisible God, the express image of His person, and the true preservative against all idolatry, when truly known. Build yourselves deep down on the strong foundation of His finished work upon the cross. Settle it firmly in your mind, that Christ Jesus has done everything needful in order to present you without spot before the throne of God, and that simple, childlike faith on your part is the only thing required to give you an entire interest in the work of Christ. Settle it firmly in your mind, that having this faith, you are completely justified in the sight of God, will never be more justified if you live to the age of Methuselah, and do the works of the Apostle Paul, and

can add nothing to that complete justification by any acts, deeds, works, performances, fastings, prayers, almsdeeds, attendance on ordinances or anything else of you own.

And oh! keep up, keep up, I beseech you, continual communion with the person of the Lord Jesus. Abide in Him daily, feed on Him daily, look to Him daily, lean on Him daily, live upon Him daily, draw from His fulness daily. Realise this, and the idea of other mediators, other comforters, other intercessors, will seem utterly absurd. 'What need is there?' you will reply, 'I have Christ, and in Him I have all.'

Brethren, let the Lord Christ have His rightful place in your heart, and all other things in your religion will soon fall into their right places also; Church, ministers, sacraments, ordinances, all will go down, and take the second place.

Except Christ sits as Priest and King upon the throne of your heart, that little kingdom within will be in perpetual confusion. But only let Him be all in all there and I have no fear for you. Before Him every idol, every Dragon shall fall down.

5

SCATTERED ISRAEL TO BE GATHERED

Hear the Word of the Lord, O ye nations, and declare it in the isles afar off, and say, he that scattered Israel will gather him, and keep him, as a shepherd doth his flock (Jer. 31:10).

The text which heads this page is singularly full and comprehensive. It contains both history and prophecy. It speaks of the scattering of Israel; this is history. It speaks of the gathering of Israel; this is prophecy. It demands the attention both of the Jew and the Gentile. To the Jew it holds out a hope: 'Israel,' it says, 'shall be gathered.' On the Gentile it lays a command: 'Hear the Word of the Lord,' it says, 'O ye nations, and declare it in the isles afar off: He that scattered Israel will gather him.'

Reader, the whole body of Gentile Christendom is specially addressed in this text. There is no evading this conclusion on any fair interpretation of Scripture. We ourselves are among the nations to whom Jeremiah speaks. Upon us devolves a portion of the duty which he here sets forth. The text is the Lord's voice to all the Churches of Christ among the Gentiles. It is a voice to the churches of England, Scotland and Ireland. It is a voice to the churches of Germany, Switzerland, Sweden, Holland, Denmark and America. It is a voice to all Christendom. And what does the voice say? It bids us proclaim far and wide the will of God concerning the Jewish nation. It bids us keep one another in memory of God's past and future dealings with Israel. 'He that scattered Israel will gather him.'

Reader, I ask your serious attention for a few minutes, while I try to place the Jewish subject before you in a connected and condensed form. I propose in this address to show you from Scripture the past, the present and future of Israel. I know few texts in the Bible which contain such a complete summary of the subject as the one before you. This text I shall endeavour to unfold.

I entreat you not to dismiss the subject as speculative, fanciful and unprofitable. The world is growing old. The last days are come upon us. The foundations of the earth are out of course. The ancient institutions of society are wearing out and going to pieces. The end of all things is at hand. Surely it becomes a wise man, at a time like this, to turn to the pages of prophecy, and to inquire what is yet to come. At a time like this the declarations of God concerning His people Israel ought to be carefully weighed and examined. 'At the time of the end,' says Daniel, 'the wise shall understand' (Dan. 12:10).

There are four points on which I purpose to dwell, in considering the words of Jeremiah which stand at the head of this address.

1. The meaning of the word Israel, both here and elsewhere in Scripture.
2. The present condition of Israel.
3. The future prospects of Israel.
4. The duty which Gentile churches owe to Israel.

1. The meaning of the word *Israel*. The definition of terms is of first importance in theology. Unless we explain the meaning of the words we use in our religious statements, our arguments are often wasted, and we seem like men beating the air.

The word 'Israel' is used nearly seven hundred times in the Bible. I can only discover three senses in which it is used. First, it is one of the names of Jacob, the father of the twelve tribes; a name specially given to him by God. Secondly, it is a name given to the ten tribes which separated from Judah and Benjamin in the days of Rehoboam, and became a distinct kingdom. This kingdom is often called Israel in contradistinction to the kingdom of Judah. Thirdly and lastly, it is a name given to the whole Jewish nation, to all members of the twelve tribes which sprung from Jacob, and were brought out of Egypt into the land of Canaan. This is by far the most common signification of the word in the Bible. It is the only signification in which I can find the word 'Israel' used throughout the whole New Testament. It is the same in which the word is used in the text which I am considering this day. That Israel, which God has scattered and will yet gather again, is the whole Jewish nation.

Now, why do I dwell upon this point? To some readers it may appear mere waste of time and words to say much about it. The things I have been saying sound to them like truisms. That Israel means Israel is a matter on which they never felt a doubt. If this be the mind of any into whose hands this address has fallen, I am thankful for it. But unhappily there are many Christians who do not see the subject with your eyes. For their sakes I must dwell on this point a little longer.

For many centuries there has prevailed in the Churches of Christ a strange, and to my mind, an unwarrantable mode of dealing with this word 'Israel'. It has been interpreted in many passages of the Psalms and Prophets, as if it meant nothing more than Christian believers. Have promises been held out to Israel? Men have been told continually that they are addressed to Gentile saints. Have glorious things been described as laid up in store for Israel? Men have been incessantly told that they describe the victories and triumphs of the gospel in Christian churches. The proofs of these things are too many to require quotation. No man can read the immense majority of commentaries and popular hymns without seeing this system of interpretation to which I now refer. Against that system I have long protested, and I hope I shall always protest as long as I live.

I do not deny that Israel was a peculiar typical people, and that God's relations to Israel were meant to be a type of His relations to His believing people all over the world.

I do not forget that it is written, 'As face answereth to face, so does the human heart of man to man'(Prov. 27:19), and that whatever spiritual truths are taught in prophecy concerning Israelitish hearts, are applicable to the hearts of Gentiles.

I would have it most distinctly understood that God's dealings with individual Jews and Gentiles are precisely one and the same. Without repentance, faith in Christ and holiness of heart, no individual Jew or Gentile shall ever be saved.

What I protest against is, the habit of allegorising plain sayings of the Word of God concerning the future history of the *nation* Israel, and explaining away the fullness of their contents in order to accommodate them to the Gentile Church. I believe the habit to be unwarranted by anything in Scripture, and to draw after it a long train of evil consequences.

Where, I would venture to ask, in the whole New Testament, shall we find any plain authority for applying the word 'Israel' to any one but the nation Israel? I can find none. On the contrary, I observe that when the Apostle Paul quotes Old Testament prophecies about the privileges of the Gentiles in gospel times, he is careful to quote texts which specifically mention the 'Gentiles' by name. The fifteenth chapter of the Epistle to the Romans is a striking illustration of what I mean. We are often told in the New Testament that, under the gospel, believing Gentiles are 'fellow heirs and partakers of the same hope' with believing Jews (Eph. 3:6). But that believing Gentiles may be called 'Israelites', I cannot see anywhere at all.

To what may be attributed that loose system of interpreting the language of the Psalms and Prophets, and the extravagant expectations of the universal conversion of the world by the preaching of the gospel, which may be observed in many Christian writers? To nothing so much, I believe, as to the habit of inaccurately interpreting the word 'Israel' and to the consequent application of promises to the Gentile churches, with which they have nothing to do. The least errors in theology always bear fruit. Never does man take up an incorrect principle of interpreting Scripture without that principle entailing awkward consequences and colouring the whole tone of his religion.

Reader, I leave this part of my subject here. I am sure that its importance cannot be overrated. In fact, a right understanding of it lies at the very root of the whole Jewish subject, and of the prophecies concerning the Jews. The duty which Christians owe to Israel, as a nation, will never be clearly understood until Christians clearly see the place that Israel occupies in Scripture.

Before going any further, I will ask all readers of this address one plain practical question. I ask you to consider calmly what sense you put on such words as 'Israel', 'Jacob' and the like, when you meet with them in the Psalms and Prophecies of the Old Testament? There are many who search the Scriptures regularly, and read through the Psalms and the Prophets once, if not twice, every year they live. Of course you attach some meaning to the words I have just referred to. You place some sense upon them. Now what is that sense? What is that meaning? Take heed that it is the right one.

Reader, accept a friendly exhortation this day. Cleave to the literal sense of Bible words, and beware of departing from it, except in cases of absolute necessity. Beware of that system of allegorising and spiritualising, and accommodating, which the school of Origen first brought in, and which has found such an unfortunate degree of favour in the Church. In reading the Authorised Version of the English Bible, do not put too much confidence in the 'headings' of pages and 'tables of contents' at beginnings of chapters, which I take leave to consider a most unhappy accompaniment of that admirable translation. Remember that those headings and tables of contents were drawn up by uninspired hands. In reading the Prophets, they are sometimes not helps but real hindrances, and less likely to assist a reader, than to lead him astray. Settle it in your mind, in reading the Psalms and Prophets that Israel means Israel, and Zion Zion, and Jerusalem Jerusalem. And, finally, whatever edification you derive from applying to your own soul the words which God addresses to His ancient people, never lose sight of the primary sense of the text.

2. The second point in the text on which I propose to dwell, is *the present condition of Israel.*

The expression used by Jeremiah describes exactly the state in which the Jews are at this day, and have been for nearly eighteen hundred years. They are a 'scattered' people. The armies of Assyria, Babylon and Rome, have, one after another, swept over the land of Israel, and carried its inhabitants into captivity. Few, if any, of the ten tribes appear to have returned from the Assyrian captivity. Not fifty thousand of Judah and Benjamin came back from the captivity of Babylon. From the last and worst captivity, when the temple was burned and Jerusalem destroyed, there has been no return at all. For eighteen hundred years Israel has been dispersed over the four quarters of the globe. Like the wreck of some goodly ship, the Jews have been tossed to and fro on all waters, and stranded in broken pieces on every shore.

But though Israel has been 'scattered', Israel has not been destroyed. For eighteen hundred years the Jews have continued a separate people, without a king, without a land, without a territory, but never lost, never absorbed among other nations. They have been often trampled under foot, but never shaken from the faith of their fathers. They have been often persecuted but never destroyed. At this very moment they are as distinct and peculiar a people as any people upon earth, an unanswerable argument in the way of the infidel, a puzzling difficulty in the way of politicians, a standing lesson to all the world. Romans, Danes, Saxons, Normans, Belgians, French and Germans have all in turn settled on English soil. All have in turn lost their national distinctiveness. All have in turn become part and parcel of the English nation, after the lapse of a few hundred years.

But it has never been so with the Jews. Dispersed as they are, there is a principle of cohesion among them which no circumstances have been able to melt. Scattered as they are, there is a national vitality among them which is stronger than that of any nation on earth. Go where you will, you will always find them. Settle where you please, in hot countries or in cold, you will find the Jews. But go where you will, and settle where you please, this wonderful people is always the same. Scattered as they are, few in number compared to those among whom they live, the Jews are always the Jews. Three thousand years ago Balaam said, 'The people shall dwell alone, and not be reckoned among the nations.' Eighteen hundred years ago our Lord said, 'This generation shall not pass away till all be fulfilled.' We see these words made good before our eyes (Num. 23:9 Luke 21:32).

But by whose hands was this scattering of Israel wrought? The text before us today declares expressly that it was the hand of God. It was not the armies of Tiglath-Pileser or Shalmanezer, of Nebuchadnezzar or Titus. They were only instruments in the hand of a far higher power. It was that God who ordereth things in heaven and earth, who dispersed the twelve tribes over the face of the earth. It was the same God who brought Israel out of Egypt with a high hand mighty arm, and planted them in Canaan, who plucked them up by the roots and made them 'wanderers among the nations' (Hosea 9:17).

And why did god send this heavy judgment upon Israel? To what are we to attribute this marvellous dispersion of a people so highly favoured? The inquiry is a very useful one. Let us mark well the answer.

The Jews are a 'scattered' people because of their many sins. Their hardness and stiffneckedness, their impenitence and unbelief, their abuse of privileges and neglect of gifts, their rejection of prophets and messengers from heaven, and finally their refusal to receive the Lord Jesus Christ, the King's own Son, these were the things which called down God's wrath upon them. These were the causes of their present dispersion. The vine which was brought out of Egypt bore wild grapes. The husbandmen to whom the vineyard was let out rendered not of the fruit to the Lord of the vineyard. The people that were brought out of the house of bondage rebelled against Him by whom they were set free. Hence the wrath of God rose until there was no remedy. Thus He says, 'You only have I known of all the inhabitants of the earth, therefore I will punish you, for all your iniquities' (Amos 3:2). 'They killed the Lord Jesus and their own prophets: they persecuted the apostles: they pleased not God: they were contrary to all men: they forbade us to speak to the Gentiles that they might be saved: and therefore the wrath has come upon them to the uttermost' (1 Thess. 2:15).

Israel was 'scattered' to be a perpetual warning to the Gentile Churches of God. The Jews are God's beacon or pillar of salt to all Christendom and a silent standing lesson which all who profess to know God ought never to forget. They proclaim to all Christians God's hatred of spiritual pride and self-righteousness, God's high displeasure with those who exalt the traditions of men and depart from the Word, God's hatred of formality and ceremonialism. If any man desires to know how much God hates these things, he has only to look at the present condition of the Jews. For eighteen hundred years God has held them up before the eyes of the world, and written His abhorrence of their sins in letters which he who runs may read.

I cannot pass away from this part of my subject without entreating all who read this address to learn a practical lesson from the scattering of Israel. I entreat you to remember the causes which led to their dispersion, and to beware of the slightest approach to their peculiar sins. I am sure the warning is needed in these latter days. I am sure that the opinions which are boldly broached and openly maintained by many religious teachers in all churches of Christendom call loudly on all Christians to stand on their guard. It is not without good reason that our Lord said, 'Take heed and beware of the leaven of the Sadducees and Pharisees' (Matt. 16:6). Look to your own heart. Beware of tampering with false doctrines. Churches are never safe unless their members know their individual responsibility. Let us each look to ourselves, and take heed to our own souls. The same God lives who scattered Israel because of Israel's sins. And what says He to the Churches of Christ this day? He says, 'Be not high-minded, but fear. If God spared not the natural branches, take heed lest He also spare not thee' (Rom. 11:20, 21).

3. The third part of the text on which I propose to dwell is *the future prospects of Israel.*

In taking up this branch of my subject, I feel that I am entering on the region of unfulfilled prophecy. I desire to do so with all reverence, and with a deep sense of the many difficulties surrounding this department of theology, and the many diversities of opinion which prevail upon it. But the servant of God must call no man master on earth. Truth is never likely to be attained unless all ministers of Christ speak out their opinions fully, freely and unreservedly, and give men an opportunity of weighing what they teach.

Reader, however great the difficulties surrounding many parts of unfulfilled prophecy, two points appear to my own mind to stand out as plainly as if written by a sunbeam. One of these points is the second personal advent of our Lord Jesus Christ before the Millennium. The other of these points is the future literal gathering of the Jewish nation, and their restoration to their own land. I tell no man that these two truths are essential to salvation, and that he cannot be saved except he sees them with my eyes. But I tell any man that these truths appear to me distinctly set down in holy

Scripture and that the denial of them is as astonishing and incomprehensible to my own mind as the denial of the divinity of Christ.

Now what says our text about the future prospects of the Jews? It says, 'He that scattered Israel will gather him'. That gathering is an event which plainly is yet to come. It could not apply in any sense to the ten tribes of Israel. They have never been gathered in any way. Their scattering has never come to an end. It cannot be applied to the return of the remnant of Judah and Benjamin from the Babylonish captivity. The language of the text makes such an application impossible. The text is addressed to the Gentiles, 'the nations'. The declaration they are commanded to make is 'to the isles of the sea'. In the days of the Babylonish captivity, the nations of the earth knew nothing of the Word of the LORD. They were sunk in darkness, and had not even heard the LORD's name. If Jeremiah had told them to proclaim the return of the Jews from Babylon under such circumstances it would have been useless and absurd. There is but one fair and legitimate interpretation of the promise of the text. The event it declares is yet future. The gathering spoken of is a gathering which is yet to come.

Reader, I believe that the interpretation I have just given is in entire harmony with many other plain prophecies of Scripture. Time would fail me if I were to quote a tenth part of the texts which teach the same truth. Out of the sixteen prophets of the Old Testament, there are at least ten in which the gathering and restoration of the Jews in the latter days are expressly mentioned. From each of these ten I will take one testimony. I say 'one' testimony deliberately. I am anxious not to overload the subject with evidence. I would only remind the reader that the texts I am about to quote are only a small portion of the evidence that might be brought forward.

Hear what Isaiah says (11:11, 12): 'It shall come to pass in that day, that the Lord shall set His hand again the second time to recover the remnant of His people, which shall be left, from Assyria, and from Egypt, and from Pathros, and from Cush, and from Elam, and from Shinar, and from Hamath, and from the islands of the sea. And He shall set up an ensign for the nations, and shall assemble the outcasts of Israel, and gather together the dispersed of Judah from the four corners of the earth.'

Hear what Ezekiel says (37:21): 'Thus saith the LORD God: Behold, I will take the children of Israel from among the heathen, whither they be gone, and will gather them on every side, and bring them into their own land.'

Hear what Hosea says (1:11; 3:4, 5): 'Then shall the children of Judah and the children of Israel be gathered together, and appoint themselves one head, and they shall come up out of the land: for great shall be the day of Jezreel.'... 'For the children of Israel shall abide many days without a king, and without a prince, and without a sacrifice, and without an image, and without an ephod, and without teraphim: afterward shall the children of Israel return, and seek the LORD their God, and David their king: and shall fear the LORD and His goodness in the latter days.'

Hear what Joel says (3:20): 'But Judah shall dwell for ever, and Jerusalem from generation to generation.'

Hear what Amos says (9: 14, 15): 'And I will bring again the captivity of my people of Israel, and they shall build the waste cities, and inhabit them; and they shall plant vineyards, and drink the wine thereof; they shall also make gardens, and eat the fruit of them. And I will plant them upon their land, and they shall no more be pulled up out of their land which I have given them, saith the LORD they God.'

Hear what Obadiah says (1:17): 'But upon Mount Zion shall be deliverance, and there shall be holiness: and the house of Jacob shall possess their possessions.'

Hear what Micah says (4:6, 7): 'In that day, says the Lord, will I assemble her that halteth, and I will gather her that is driven out, and her that I have afflicted: and I will make her that halted a remnant, and her that was cast far off a strong nation: and the LORD shall reign over them in Mount Zion from henceforth, even for ever.'

Hear what Zephaniah says (3:14-20): 'Sing, O daughter of Zion; shout O Israel; be glad and rejoice with all thy heart, O daughter of Jerusalem. The LORD hath taken away thy judgments, He hath cast out thine enemy; the King of Israel, even the LORD, is in the midst of thee: thou shalt not see evil any more. In that day it shall be said to Jerusalem, Fear thou not: and to Zion, Let not thine hands be slack. The LORD thy God in the midst of thee is mighty; He will save, he will rejoice over thee with joy; He will rest in His love, he will joy over thee with singing. I will gather them that are sorrowful for the solemn assembly, who are of thee to whom the reproach of it was a burden. Behold, at that time I will undo all that afflict thee: and I will save her that halteth, and gather her that was driven out; and I will get them praise and fame in every land where they had been put to shame. At that time will I bring you again, even in the time that I gather you: for I will make you a name and a praise among all people of the earth, when I turn back your captivity before your eyes, saith the LORD.'

Hear what Zechariah says (10:6-10): 'And I will strengthen the house of Judah, and I will save the house of Joseph, and I will bring them again to place them; for I have mercy upon them: and they shall be as though I had not cast them off: for I am the LORD their God and will hear them. And they of Ephraim shall be like a mighty man, and their heart shall rejoice as through wine: yea, their children shall see it and be glad; their heart shall rejoice in the LORD. I will hiss for them, and gather them; for I have redeemed them: and they shall increase as they have increased. And I will sow them among the people: and they shall remember me in far countries; and they shall live with their children and turn again. I will bring them again also out of the land of Egypt, and gather them out of Assyria; and I will bring them into the land of Gilead and Lebanon; and a place shall not be found for them.'

Hear, lastly, what Jeremiah says (30: 3, 11): 'For, lo, the days come, saith the LORD, that I will bring again the captivity of my people Israel and Judah, saith the LORD: and I will cause them to return to the land that I gave to their fathers, and they shall possess it.'... 'For I am with thee, saith the LORD, to save thee: though I make a full end of all nations whither I have scattered thee, yet will I not make a full end of thee; but I will correct thee in measure, and will not leave thee altogether unpunished.'

Reader, I place these texts before you without note or comment. I only wish that they may be weighed and examined, and the several chapters from which they are taken read carefully. I believe there is one common remark that applies to them all. They all point to a time which is yet future. They all predict the final gathering of the Jewish nation from the four quarters of the globe, and their restoration to their own land.

I must ask you to believe that the subject admits of being drawn out at far greater length than the limits of this address allow. I am resolved, however, not to encumber it by entering on topics of comparatively subordinate importance. I will not complicate it by dwelling on the manner in which Israel shall be gathered, and the particular events which shall accompany the gathering. I might show you by scriptural evidence that the Jews will probably first be gathered in an unconverted state, though humbled, and will afterwards be taught to look to Him whom they have pierced, through much tribulation. I might speak of the future glory of Jerusalem, after the Jews are restored, and the last siege which it shall endure: as described by Zechariah and by our Lord Jesus Christ. But I forbear. I will not travel beyond the bounds of my text. I think it is better to present its weighty promise to you in its naked simplicity. 'Israel scattered shall yet be gathered.' This is the future prospect of the Jew.

Now is there anything *contrary to this gathering in the New Testament?* I cannot find a single word. So far from this being the case, I find a chapter in the Epistle to the Romans where the subject is fully discussed. An inspired

Apostle speaks there of Israel being once more 'received' into God's favour, 'grafted' and 'saved' (see Rom. 11:15-32).

Is there anything *impossible* in this gathering of Israel? Who talks of impossibilities? If an infidel, let him explain the present condition and past history of Israel, if he can; and when he has solved that mighty problem, we may listen to him. If a Christian, let him think again before he talks of anything being impossible with God. Let him read the vision of the dry bones in Ezekiel, and mark to whom that vision applies. Let him look to his own conversion and resurrection from the death of trespasses and sins, and recall the unworthy thought that anything is too hard for the Lord.

Is there anything *inconsistent with God's former dealings* in the gathering of Israel? Is there any extravagance in expecting such an event? Why should we say so? Reasoning from analogy, I can see no ground for refusing to believe that God may yet do wonderful things for the Jewish people. It would not be more marvellous to see them gathered once more into Palestine, than it was to see them brought from Egypt into the promised land. What God has done once, He may surely do again.

Is there anything *improbable* in the gathering of Israel? Alas! reader, we are poor judges of probabilities. God's way of carrying into effect His own purposes are not to be judged by man's standard, or measured by the line and plummet of what man calls probable. In the day when the children of Israel went forth from Egypt, would any one have said it was *probable* that such a nation of serfs would ever produce a book that should turn the world upside down? Yet that nation has done it. From that nation has come the Bible. Four thousand years ago, would any one have said it was *probable* that God's Son would come to earth, and suffer in the flesh on the cross, before He came to earth in glory to reign? Yet so it has been. Christ has lived, and Christ has suffered, and Christ has died. Away with this talk about improbabilities. The ways of God are not our ways.

Finally, is there anything *fanatical or enthusiastic* in this expectation that Israel shall be gathered? Why should men say so? Your own eyes tell you that the present order of things will never convert the world. There is not a church, or a parish, or a congregation, where the converted are more than a little flock. There is not a faithful minister on earth, and never has been, who has ever seen more than the 'taking out of a people' to serve Christ. A change must come before the earth shall be filled with the knowledge of the Lord. A new order of teachers must be raised up, and a new dispensation ushered in. These teachers, I firmly believe, shall be converted Jews. And then shall be seen the fulfilment of the remarkable words, 'If the casting of them away be the reconciling of the world, what shall the receiving of them be, but life from the dead? (Rom. 11:15).

I may not dwell longer on this branch of my subject. I leave it with one general remark, which may sound to some readers like a bald truism. Whether it be a truism or not, I believe the remark to be of vital importance, and I heartily wish that it was more deeply impressed on all our minds.

I ask you, then, to settle it firmly in your mind, that when God says a thing shall be done, we ought to believe it. We have no right to begin talking of probable and improbable, like and unlikely, possible and impossible, reasonable and unreasonable. What is all this but veiled scepticism, and infidelity in disguise? What hath the Lord said? And what hath the Lord spoken? What saith the Scriptures? What is written in the Word? These are the only questions we have a right to ask; and when the answer to them is plain, we have nothing to do but believe. Our reason may rebel. Our preconceived ideas of what God ought to do may receive a rude shock. Our private systems of prophetical interpretation may be shattered to pieces. Our secret prejudices may be grievously offended. But what are we to do? We must abide by Scripture, or be of all men most miserable. At any cost let us cling to the Word. 'Let God be true, and every man a liar.'

In all matters of unfulfilled prophecy, I desire, for my own part, to fall back on this principle. I see many things I cannot explain. I find many difficulties I cannot solve. But I dare not give up my principle. I am determined to believe everything that God says. I know it will all prove true at the last day. I read that He says in the text before us this day, 'He that scattered Israel shall gather him'. It must be true, I feel, whatever be the difficulties. That Israel shall be gathered, I steadfastly believe.

4. The last point on which I propose to dwell is one purely practical. It is the duty which Gentile churches owe to Israel.

Reader, in touching on this point, I would not have you for a moment suppose that the future gathering of Israel depends on anything that man can do. God's counsels and purposes are independent of human strength. The sun will set tonight at its appointed hour, and neither Queen, Lords, nor Commons, Pope, Presidents, nor Emperors, can hasten, prevent or put off its setting. The tides of the sea will ebb and flow this week in their regular course, and no scientific decree nor engineering skill can interfere with their motion. And just in like manner the promises of God concerning

Israel will all be fulfilled in due season, whether we will hear or whether we will forbear. When the 'times and seasons' arrive which God has 'put in His own power', Israel will be gathered; and all the alliances and combinations of statesmen, and all the persecution and unbelief of apostate churches, shall not be able to prevent it.

But seeing that we look for such things, it becomes us all to be found in the path of duty. It behoves us to consider gravely the solemn question, What manner of persons ought we to be? And in what way can we testify our full assent to God's purposes about the Jews? Can we in no sense be fellow workers with God? Should we not remember that remarkable saying of St. Paul, 'Through your mercy they shall obtain mercy' (Rom. 11:31). This is the question to which I now desire briefly to supply a practical answer.

1. I believe then, for one thing, that it is a duty incumbent on all Gentile Christians *to take a special interest* in the spiritual conversion of the Jewish nation, and to give their conversion a special place in our prayers. I say, advisedly, their spiritual condition. I leave alone their civil and political position. I speak, exclusively, of our duty to Jewish souls. I say that we owe them a special debt, and that this debt ought to be carefully paid.

We prize our Bibles and we are right to do so. A heaven without a sun would not be more blank than a world without a Bible. But do we ever reflect that every page in that blessed Book was written under God's inspiration by Israelitish hands? Remember that every chapter and verse you read in your Bible you owe under God to Israel. There is not a religious society that meets in London in the month of May which is not constantly working with Israelitish tools.

We prize the glorious gospel of the grace of God, and we are right to do so. A land without the gospel, like Tartary and China, is nothing better than a moral wilderness. See the vast difference between Europe and America with the gospel, notwithstanding all their vices, and Africa and Asia without it. But do we ever reflect that the first preachers of that gospel were all Jews. The men who, at cost of their lives, first carried from town to town the blessed tidings of Christ crucified, were not Gentiles. The first to take up the lamp of truth, which was passed from hand to hand, till it reached our heathen forefathers, were all men of Israel.

We rejoice in Christ Jesus, and glory in His person and work. Well may we do so! Without a living Saviour, and the blood of His atonement once made on the cross, we should indeed be miserable. But do we ever reflect that when that Saviour became a man, in order that, as man's substitute, He might live, and suffer and die, He was born of a Jewish woman! Yes! let that never be forgotten. When 'God was manifest in the flesh' and was 'born of a woman', that woman was a virgin of the house of David. When the promised Saviour took flesh and blood that He might bruise the serpent's head and redeem man, He took not flesh and blood of any royal house among the Gentiles, but of one of the twelve tribes of Israel.

Reader, I know well that these are ancient things. They have often been urged, often alleged, often pressed on the attention of the churches. I am not ashamed to bring them forward again. I say, that if there be such a thing as gratitude in heart of man, it is the duty of all Gentile Christians to take special interest in the work of doing good to the Jews.

2. I believe, futhermore, that it is a duty incumbent on all Gentile Christians to be specially careful that they *take up stumbling-blocks out of the way of Israel* and to see that they do nothing to disgust them with Christianity, or hinder their conversion. This is a matter which is expressly mentioned in Scripture. There we find Isaiah bidding us, 'Take up the stumbling-blocks out of the way of God's people' (Isa. 57:14). Truly the Prophet might well speak of this. No man can look round the Gentile churches and fail to see that he had cause.

What shall we say of the glaring unholiness and neglect of God's Ten Commandments which prevail so widely in Christendom? What shall we say of the open unblushing idolatry which offends the eye in all Roman Catholic churches? What shall we say of the widespread habit of Sabbath breaking which is eating like a cancer into the heart of the Protestant churches? What shall we say of the rationalistic mode of interpreting Old Testament history, which has crept so extensively into modern commentaries, the system of regarding the histories of Abraham, and Jacob, and Joseph, and the like, as so many myths, or ingenious fables, but not as narratives of facts which really took place? What shall we say of the traditional mode of interpreting Old Testament prophecies, in which so many Christians indulge? The system of appropriating all the blessings to the Church of Christ, and handing over all the bitter things to poor despised Israel, the system of interpreting all prophecies about Christ's first advent literally, and all prophecies about His second advent figuratively, requiring the Jew to believe the first in the letter, and refusing in turn to believe the second, except in what is called, by a sad misnomer, a *spiritual* sense? What shall we say of all these things, but that they are stumbling-blocks, great stumbling-blocks, in the way of the conversion of the Jews? What are they all but great barriers between the Jew and Christ, and barriers cast up by Christian hands?

Reader, we must all do our part in aiding to take these stumbling-blocks away. Here at least all may help. Here, at any rate, every Gentile Christian can aid the Jewish cause. The more pure and lovely we can make our holy faith, the more we are likely to recommend it to Israel. The more we can check the progress of the Roman apostasy, and protest against its idolatries and corruptions, the more likely is the Jew to believe there is something in Christianity. The more we can promote the habit of taking all Scripture in its plain literal sense, the more we are likely to remove prejudices in the minds of honest inquirers in Israel, and to make them ready to hear what we have to say.

3. Finally, I believe it is a duty incumbent on all Gentile Christians, to *use special efforts to promote the conversion of the Jews*. I say special efforts advisedly. The Jews are a peculiar people and must be approached in a peculiar way.

They are peculiar in their state of mind. They require an entirely different treatment from the heathen. Their objections are not the heathen man's objections. Their difficulties are not the heathen man's difficulties. They believe many things which the heathen man never heard of. They have a standard of right and wrong with which the heathen man is utterly unacquainted. Like the heathen they need to be converted. Like the heathen they need to be brought to Christ. But the lines of argument to be pursued with the Jew and the heathen are widely dissimilar. A faithful missionary might do admirably well among the heathen, who might find it difficult to reason with a Jew.

They are peculiar in their position in the world. They are not to be found all assembled together, like the Africans at Sierra Leone, or the Hindus, or New Zealanders, or Chinese. They are emphatically a scattered people, a few in one country, and a few in another. An effort to get at them must aim at nothing short of sending missionaries in search of them all over the world.

Circumstances like these appear to me point out clearly that nothing less than a special effort will ever enable Christians to discharge their debt to Israel. There must be a division of labour in the missionary field. There must be a special concentration of preaching, praying and loving intercourse on the Jewish people, or the churches of the Gentiles can never expect to do them much spiritual good. Without such special effort the cause of Israel will inevitably be lost sight of in the cause of the whole heathen world. Without such *special* effort I cannot see how the command of the text can be rightly obeyed.

Now here lies the claim which the Society for Promoting Christianity amongst the Jews makes on English Christians in the present day for aid. It enables them to make a special effort on behalf of Israel. It supplies them with an outgate for their sympathy, and a faithful instrumentality for sending the gospel to God's ancient people. It is in this light that I earnestly commend the Society to the support of all who love the Lord Jesus Christ in sincerity, and desire to do good in the world.

I am quite aware that it is a common remark, that the Society does nothing. Its results appear to some very small and insignificant. I think, however, that those who make such an objection, have probably never considered the very peculiar character of the work which the Society does. Its field is necessarily a singularly scattered one. Its agents are necessarily scattered widely apart one from another. The work that they do, in the very nature of things, makes far less show than the work of a united band of missionaries at Tinnevelly or Sierra Leone. Tried, I believe, by any fair standard, the work of the Society for Promoting Christianity amongst the Jews has no cause to fear inspection. Its agents are bearing a testimony in some places, and awakening in Israel thought, reflection and inquiry. In others they are gradually softening prejudices, and inclining Jews to hold discussions or listen to gospel statements. In others they are calling out a people, and leading them to the foot of the cross. What more do we see going on at home? What greater results than these can be found in any congregation on earth where the gospel is preached? And, after all, duties are ours, and the results are God's.

I leave the whole subject with three remarks, which I pray God to impress on the minds of all into whose hands this address may fall.

1. For one thing, I charge every reader of this address to remember the special blessing which God has promised to all who care for Israel. Whatever a sneering world may say, the Jews are a people 'beloved for their father's sake'. Of Jerusalem it is written, 'They shall prosper that love thee' (Ps. 122:6). Of Israel it is written, 'Blessed is he that blesseth thee, and cursed is he that curseth thee' (Num. 24:9). These promises are not yet exhausted. We see their fulfilment in the blessing granted to the Church of England since the day when the Jewish cause was first taken up. We see

their fulfilment in the peculiar honour which God has put from time to time on individual Christians who have laboured especially for the Jewish cause. Charles Simeon, Edward Bickersteth, Robert M'Cheyne, Haldane Stewart and Dr. Marsh, are striking examples of what I mean. Is there any one that desires God's special blessing? Then let him labour in the cause of Israel, and he shall not fail to find it.

2. For another thing, I charge every reader of this address never to forget the close connection which Scripture reveals between the time of Israel's gathering and the time of Christ's second advent to the world. In one Psalm it is expressly declared, 'When the Lord shall build up Zion, He shall appear in His glory' (102:16). Where is the true believer that does not long for that blessed day. Where is the true Christian that does not cry from the bottom of his heart, 'Thy kingdom come'? Let all such, work, and give, and pray, so that the gospel may have free course in Israel and be glorified. The time to favour Zion is closely bound up with the restitution of all things. Blessed indeed is that work of which the completion shall usher in the second coming of the Lord!

3. Finally, I charge every reader of this address to make sure work of his own salvation. Rest not in mere head-knowledge of prophetical subjects. Be not content with intellectual soundness in the faith. Give diligence to make your own calling and election sure. Seek to know that your repentance and faith are genuine and true. Seek to feel that you are one with Christ and Christ in you; and that you are washed, sanctified and justified. Then, whether the completion of God's promises to Israel be near or far off, your own portion will be sure. You will 'stand in your lot' safely, when the kingdoms of this world are passing away. You will meet Christ without fear when He comes the second time to Zion. You will join boldly in the song, 'Blessed is He that cometh in the name of the Lord'. You will sit down with Abraham, Isaac and Jacob, in the kingdom of God, and go out no more.[5]

6

THE READING WHICH IS BLESSED

The Revelation of Jesus Christ, which God gave unto him, to shew unto his servants things which must shortly come to pass; and he sent and signified it by his angel unto his servant John; who bare record of the word of God, and of the testimony of Jesus Christ, and of all things that he saw. Blessed is he that readeth, and they that hear the words of this prophecy, and keep those things which are written therein: for the time is at hand (Rev. 1:1-3).

We live in 'troublous' and 'perilous' times. It is many years since there has been so much in the aspect of public affairs to raise anxious thoughts, as there is in the present day. We are always apt to exaggerate the importance of events that happen in our own days. I do not forget that. But I cannot retract what I have just written. I look around me at the things now going on in the Church and in the world. I look forward to the possible future. And as I look, I feel that I am justified in speaking of our times as 'perilous' and 'troublous'. I appeal to the judgment of all who observe the history of their own times. *Is there not a cause?*

'Here are three heavy judgments which God can send upon a nation – the sword, the pestilence and the famine. All these three have fallen heavily upon our country within the last few years. The Irish famine, the Russian war, the cholera, the cattle plague, have left marks on this country which cannot be erased. Surely these signs of the times deserve no common notice. They should make us say with Habakkuk, 'I will stand upon my watch, and set me upon my tower, and will watch to see what He will say unto me' (Hab. 2:1). They should make us cry with Daniel, 'O my Lord, what shall be the end of these things?' (Dan. 12:8).

But one thing, at all events, is clear, and that is the duty incumbent on Christians to search more diligently than ever the *prophetical Scriptures*. Let us not be like the Jews at the first advent, blind to the hand of God and the fulfilment of His purposes in all that is going in the world. Let us rather remember that the word of prophecy is given to be 'a light shining in a dark place, until the day dawn, and the day-star arise' (2 Peter 1:19). Let us walk much in that light. Let us search 'what and what manner of time the Spirit of Christ in the Prophets did signify, when He testified before the sufferings of Christ, and the glory that should follow' (1 Peter 1:11). Let us compare prophecies fulfilled with prophecies unfulfilled, and endeavour to make the one illustrate the other. Let us strive, above all, to obtain clear views of the things yet to be expected, both in the Church and the world, before the end comes, and time shall be no more.

With such feelings I now invite you to enter on the consideration of the verses of Scripture which stand at the head of this address. Those verses, I need hardly remind you, are the preface or opening words of the book of Revelation. May the blessing which is specially promised to the readers and hearers of this book, be with all into whose hands this address may fall!

Reader, there are three points to which I desire to call your attention:

1. The general character of the book of Revelation.
2. The arguments commonly used to deter men from reading it.
3. The many useful lessons which the study of it is calculated to teach.

1. *The general character of the book of Revelation.* The book of Revelation differs widely from any other book of the Old or New Testament. In many respects it is thoroughly unlike the rest of the Bible. There is a solemn and majestic peculiarity about it. It stands alone.

It is peculiar in *the dignity with which it begins.* The very first verse prepares the reader for something extraordinary, for a book even more directly from God, if possible, than one written under the plenary inspiration of the Holy Ghost. It is called 'The Revelation of Jesus Christ, Which God gave unto Him, to shew unto His servants things which must shortly come to pass; and He sent and signified it by His angel unto His servant John'.

It is peculiar in *the subject matter which it contains.* It contains less of doctrinal and practical Christianity, in proportion to its length, than any book of the New Testament. With few exceptions, its pages are filled with prophecies, prophecies of the widest range, extending, it seems to me, from the time of John to the very end of the world; prophecies embracing a vast number of events, spreading over the whole 'times of the Gentiles' and covering the mighty interval between the destruction of the first Jerusalem and the descent of the New Jerusalem from heaven; prophecies of universal importance to all mankind, having reference not only to the condition and prospects of the believing Church, but also of the unconverted world.

It is peculiar in *the style and dress in which its subject matter is clothed.* With the exception of the second and third chapters, the greater part of the book is composed of visions which the Apostle John saw in the Spirit. In these visions the vast range of the Church's history was revealed to him under emblems, figures, allegories, symbols and similitudes. The meaning of the great majority of these symbols and emblems is not explained. The general characteristics of these visions are much alike. All are marked by a vastness, a grandeur, a majesty, a life, a force, a boldness, a sublimity, entirely unparalleled in any human writings. The door opened in heaven, the voice like a trumpet speaking, the sea of glass like crystal, the seven seals, the seven trumpets, the seven vials, the four angels holding the four winds, the mighty angel with a face like the sun, his right foot on the sea, his left on the earth, the woman clothed with the sun and the moon under her feet, the great red dragon having seven heads and ten horns, the beast that rose out of the sea, the mighty earthquake, the destruction of Babylon, the summoning of the fowls of heaven to the supper of the great God, the binding of Satan, the great white throne, the last judgment, the descent of the New Jerusalem from heaven, the description of the glorious city, who can read such things without being struck by them? Who can study them and avoid the conclusion, 'This is written with the finger of God'?

Such is the general character of the book of Revelation. Such is the book which you are emphatically told, it is 'blessed' to read. I will only offer two general remarks on the symbolical style in which the book is composed, and then pass on.

One remark is, that you must not regard the use of symbolical language as entirely peculiar to the book of Revelation. You will find it in other parts of Scripture. The very emblems and figures of the Apocalypse, whose meaning seems so obscure, are often employed by the Holy Ghost in the Old Testament. You read, for example, of four living creatures in the fourth chapter. You read of four also in Ezekiel 1:5. You read of horses in the vision of the first four seals. You read of horses also in the vision of Zechariah 6:2, 3. You read of a sealed company in the seventh chapter. You read also of a sealed and marked people in the vision of Ezekiel 9. You read of a plague of locusts under the fifth trumpet. You read of locusts also in the prophecy of Joel 2. You read of John eating the little book in the tenth chapter. You read also of Ezekiel eating the roll in his vision in chapter 3. You read of olive trees and candlesticks in the vision of the two witnesses. You read of the same emblems in the prophecy of Zechariah 4. You read of a beast having seven heads and ten horns, in the thirteenth chapter. You read of a similar beast in Daniel 7. You read of a wondrous celestial city in the twenty-first chapter. You have the description of a city scarcely less mysterious, though different, at the end of Ezekiel (40 etc)…these things are worthy of remark. They show us that we must not be stumbled by the symbols of Revelation, as if they were altogether a new and strange thing. We must remember they are used in the Old Testament as well as here, though far more sparingly, in communicating the mind of God to man. The peculiarity of the Apocalypse is not so much the use of symbols and emblems, as the profuse abundance of them.

My other remark is, that a symbolical style of composition will always seem more strange to us than it does to Oriental nations.[6] Figures, parables, illustrations and similitudes, are infinitely better known in the countries round the Holy Land than they are among ourselves.

The hieroglyphic inscriptions, for example, which abound in Egypt and elsewhere in the East, are nothing more than symbolical writings. Who does not know that at first sight these hieroglyphics seem uncouth, meaningless, dark and obscure? The first step the student of them must take is to become familiar with their appearance. By and by he may hope to become acquainted with the key to their meaning. Ultimately, that key being found, these very hieroglyphics are found full of interesting matter. It is much the same with the book of Revelation. It is a book of sacred hieroglyphics. Its very style is one to which our matter-of-fact northern mind is utterly unaccustomed. To us, therefore, its visions seem doubly strange, strange because we are not familiar with such a mode of conveying our ideas, stranger still, because in many cases we have no clue to their meaning. Our first step must be to read them and study them much, so as to become familiar with their outward garb, with the style of composition in which they are clothed. So studying in a prayerful spirit, we may hope that the meaning of their inward contents will be gradually made more plain to our minds.

One thing let us always remember in reading the visions of the Apocalypse. Whether we understand little or much, let us settle it in our minds as a fixed principle, that every vision in the book has a real definite meaning.

The time is short. We hasten on towards a day when every page shall be unfolded and unsealed. Every knot shall be untied. Every hard question shall be solved. Then shall we see that the Revelation, like every other part of the inspired volume, was all 'very good'.

Then shall we find that the blessing pronounced on its students was not given in vain, and those readers whom God blesses are blessed indeed.

2. Let us consider, in the next place, *the arguments commonly used to deter men from studying the book of Revelation.*

There never have been wanting good men who have cried down the study of Revelation as unprofitable. They have spoken of it as a book too dark and mysterious for use. They have bid men respect it as inspired but not touch it, reverence it at a distance, as part of the Bible, but not draw near to it or handle its contents. To this prejudice we probably owe the unhappy omission of the book from the daily calendar of lessons in the Liturgy of the Church of England. It is deeply to be regretted, that in the last arrangement of that calendar the Apocryphal story of Bel and the Dragon should have been thrust in and the Revelation of John the Divine should have been shut out. Room was made for an entirely uninspired composition. No place was found for a book to the reading of which a special blessing is promised. Truly we may say in this case, 'Great men are not always wise, neither do the aged understand judgment' (Job 32:9).[7]

Reader, when such prejudices have existed against the study of the book of Revelation among good men, you will not wonder that the children of the world should have gone further. Men, more witty than wise, have launched sharp sayings, jests and jibes at its students. They have not been ashamed to find a mark for witticism in its solemn and mysterious visions. Even a man like Scaliger declared that one of Calvin's wisest acts was his abstaining from writing a commentary on the book. Dr. South, a clever writer, though an unsound theologian, said that the study of Revelation either 'found a man mad or made him so.'[8]

But, after all, what is the real worth of the objections commonly made to the study of Revelation? Let us weigh them in the balances, and see to what they amount. To my own mind they appear neither so serious nor so unanswerable as is commonly supposed.

One class of objectors dislike the book because it seems to point to a coming state of things in the world, which, to their minds, *is monstrous, incredible and improbable.*

That God should send plagues and judgments upon the nations of the earth, because of their sins against Him, that the kings of the earth, and the great men, and the captains, and the rich, and the might, and the bond, and the free, should really flee to hide themselves from the wrath of the Lamb;

that the kingdoms of this world should really become the kingdoms of our God and of His Christ, that the saints of the Lord Jesus should ever reign upon the earth, and everything that defileth be cast out, all this is to their minds almost *absurd*. 'It is contrary to their common sense,' they tell us. 'It is a mark of a weak mind to believe it. It is extravagance. It is raving. It is enthusiasm. It is going back to the ranting of Fifth-Monarchy-men in the Commonwealth. It cannot be. We cannot show them the details of the mode in which all these things shall come to pass. They will not believe them. A book from which we draw such strange fanatical opinions can never be a profitable one to study.'

I am not careful as to the answer to be given to such objectors. They would do well to remember that the great leading events yet to come, to which Revelation points, are in no wise more wonderful than many which have already taken place in the world. The destruction of the old world by the flood; the wasting of Babylon, Nineveh, Tyre and Egypt; the scattering of the Jews, and their perpetual preservation, notwithstanding, as a separate people: all these were things utterly improbable at the time when they were foretold. But we know that they all came to pass. And as it has been in days gone by, so it shall be in days to come. Men, in their pride of heart, forget that in the eyes of an Eternal God the movements of the nations of the earth are but as the struggles of a few ephemeral insects. Yet a little time and despotic and constitutional governments, liberal and conservative parties, all, all shall be swept away. God has said it, and with Him nothing is impossible.

As to the *manner* in which the great events predicted in Revelation shall be brought about, we do not pretend to explain it. There are many things which we accept as facts, and yet should find it impossible to explain. We believe the creation of all things out of nothing. We believe the doctrine of the Trinity in Unity. We believe the fact of the Incarnation. But who would dare to offer an explanation of any of these great mysteries? We have a right to regard unfulfilled prophecy in the same light. We claim belief for its facts, though the mode of their accomplishments be at present hid from our eyes.

I leave this first class of objectors here. I fear the secret spring of their arguments, in too many cases, is the dislike of the natural heart to spiritual things. The heart not taught by the Holy ghost rebels against he idea of severe judgments against sin, a kingdom of Christ, a reign of the saints. And why? The plain truth is, that it is not so much the book of Revelation that such a heart really objects to, as the whole gospel of Christ, and all the counsel of God.

Another class of objectors must next be noticed. These are they who deprecate the study of Revelation because of the wide *differences which prevail in the interpretation of its contents, and the notorious mistakes into which interpreters have fallen.*

I do not for a moment pretend to deny the existence of these differences and mistakes. Some good men tell us confidently that the whole book is entirely unfulfilled. They look for an accomplishment of its visions so clear and unmistakable that there shall be no room left for doubt. Other good men assure us, with no less confidence, that the whole book is fulfilled, with the exception of a small portion at the end. A third school of expositors maintains that the Revelation is partly fulfilled and partly unfulfilled. As to the details of the book, the meaning and application of the several visions it contains, the fulfilment of times and seasons, time would fail if I were to recount the various interpretations that have been put forth, and the errors that have been committed.

Now, what shall we say to these things? What can the advocate of apocalyptic study reply to these undeniable facts?

My reply is, that the variations and mistakes in the views of interpreters constitute no argument against the study of the book itself. Because others have missed the road in searching for truth, you and I are not to give up the search altogether, and sit down in contented ignorance. Who has not heard of the extravagant and contradictory theories which astronomers, geologists and physicians have occasionally propounded in their respective sciences? Yet who would think of giving up astronomy, geology or medicine in despair, because of the conflicting tenets and avowed mistakes of their professors? Luther and Zwingli differed widely about the Lord's Supper. Cranmer and Hooper differed widely about vestments. Wesley and Toplady differed widely on predestination. Yet no one in his sense would think of giving up the study of the Christian system because these good men could not agree.

My answer furthermore is, that the very mistakes and differences of apocalyptic interpreters are not without their use. They have cleared the field in many a direction, and shown us what the Revelation does not mean. Expositors have shown in many cases the weakness of other men's interpretations, if they have not succeeded in establishing their own. To know what an unfulfilled scriptural prediction does not mean is one step towards knowing what it does. When Napoleon was overtaken by the rising tide, in a dark evening, on the sandy shore of the Red Sea, he is said to have ordered his attendants to disperse, and ride in different directions, charging each one to report as he proceeded whether the water grew shallower or deeper. There was great wisdom in that order. Each man's report was useful. The report of him who found the water deepening was in its way as useful as the report of the successful finder of the right path. It is much the same with the widely-varying expositions of Revelation. It is evident that many of them must be wrong. But all in their way have done good. There is hardly one, perhaps, which has not contributed some sparks of light.[9]

My answer besides this is, that the differences of apocalyptic interpreters, great as they undoubtedly are, are often magnified and absurdly exaggerated. The common points of agreement among expositors are more in number, and greater in importance, than men commonly suppose. Whether the seals, trumpets and vials are fulfilled or not, all students of the Revelation agree that there are judgments predicted in it on the unconverted and unbelieving. Whether days mean literal days, as some say, or years, as others say, all are agreed that the time of the wicked triumphing is defined, limited and fixed by the counsels of God. Whether the beast with horns like a lamb be the Papal power or not, nearly all are agreed that Romish apostasy is foretold in the book, and doomed. Whether Christ shall come and reign visibly on earth or not, for 1,000 or 365,000 years, all are agreed that He shall come again with power and great glory, that the kingdoms of this world shall sooner or later become the kingdoms of our God, and of His Christ, and that all believers should look and long for their Lord's return. I doubt much whether this is as much considered by the opponents of apocalyptic study as it deserves.

I grant them freely that the divergences and contrarieties of the paths drawn out by the expositors of the book are very many and very great. But I bid them remember that the great terminus towards which all their lines lead is always one and the same. Oh! that men would remember that mighty terminus, and realise the tremendous importance of the end and breaking up of all things towards which they hasten. Then would they be more anxious to study any book which handles matters like those contained in Revelation. Then would they be less ready to catch at any excuse for declining apocalyptic study.

The only remaining objection to the study of Revelation which I shall notice, is that which is drawn from *the mysterious character of a large portion of the book.*

That the Revelation is full of dark and difficult things it is of course impossible to deny. Some of its symbols and emblems the Spirit of God has thought good to interpret and explain. The seven stars, the seven candlesticks, the incense, the fine linen, the waters on which the woman sat, the woman herself, all these and a few more, are expounded, perhaps as a specimen of the kind of meaning which should be attached to the symbols of the book generally. But, after every deduction, there remain a very large number of visions and emblems which the Spirit has not thought fit to interpret. These symbols are unquestionably dark and mysterious. It is not, perhaps, saying too much to admit, that after all the attempts of commentators, ancient and modern, preterist and futurist, there are many visions and symbols of Revelation which, we must confess, we do not understand. I do not say that elaborate and learned expositions of them have not been offered, but not expositions so manifestly satisfactory that we can demand a reader's assent to them. If truth be spoken, we must allow that all the expositions of *some parts* of the Revelation are nothing better than ingenious conjectures. We admire them as we read. We are not prepared to say that they are not true, or to furnish a reason for refusing our assent. But still they fail to carry conviction with them. We somehow feel the mark is not yet hit, the spring of the lock is not yet touched, the whole truth is not yet discovered.

But I appeal to the common sense of men, and their sense of fairness, and I ask them whether they have a right to expect such a book as the book of Revelation can in the very nature of things be anything but dark and mysterious.

Here is a prophetical book which spans the mighty gulf between the end of the first century and the day of judgment, a book which was given to show God's dealings with the Church and the world during a space of well nigh two thousand years, a book which points to the rise and fall of empires and kingdoms, withal the attendant wars and tumults over a third part of the habitable globe, a book above all, which does not tell its story in simple, plain matter-of-fact narration, but clothes it in majestic visions, symbols, emblems, figures and similitudes.

Here are we reading this book during a life of three score and ten years at most, with all the cares and anxieties of this world pressing upon us, with an understanding partaking in the corruption of the fall, with a heart naturally earthly and sensual, and, even after conversion, weak and deceitful, knowing little of ourselves, knowing little of contemporary history, finding constantly how hard it is to discover the real truth about events happening in our own day. Is it likely, I ask, is it probable, is it agreeable to common sense, that such students, coming to such a book, should find it anything but mysterious, and hard to understand? Can any one doubt as to the reply?

The plain truth is, that we are like children watching some mighty building in process of erection. They see a thousand operations which they are utterly unable to comprehend or explain. They see scaffolding and stones, and iron and brick, and mortar and timber, and rubbish. They hear noise and hammering, and cutting, and chipping. It seems to their eyes a vast scene of hopeless confusion. And yet to the eye of the architect all is order, system and progress. He sees the end from the beginning. He knows exactly what is going on.

It is much the same with us in trying to pass a judgment on the application of many of the apocalyptic visions. We are like those who stand on the outward surface of a sphere. The range of our mental vision is exceedingly limited. We know so little, and see so little beyond our own circle. The very pages of history are so often full of inaccuracies and lies, that we are really very poor judges of the question, whether such and such visions have been fulfilled or no. More light, I firmly believe, may yet be expected before the end comes. Much may probably be yet unfolded and unsealed. But as to any certainty about the meaning of *all* parts of the Apocalypse, when I see how little certainty there is about anything one thousand miles from us in distance, or one hundred years in time, I own I do not look for it until the Lord comes.

And here let me turn for a moment to those who secretly wonder *why the book of Revelation was not written more plainly*, and why things of such vast interest to the Church have been purposely clothed in the mysterious garb of symbol, allegory and vision.

I might easily remind such persons of Bishop Sherlock's remark on this very point: 'To inquire why the ancient prophecies are not clearer, is like inquiring why God has not given us more reason, or made us as wise as the angels.' But I have no wish to leave them there. I would rather use an argument which has often proved satisfactory to my own mind, and silenced the speculative questionings of a curious spirit.

I ask you, then, whether you cannot see wisdom and mercy in the darkness which it has pleased God to throw around the prophetical history of His Church? You wonder in your own heart why the things to come were not more clearly revealed. But, consider for a moment how fearfully deadening and depressing it would have been to the early Christians if they had clearly seen the long ages of darkness and corruption which were to elapse before the Lord returned. Reflect for a moment how much unhappiness primitive believers were spared, by not knowing for certain the events which were to take place. If humble saints in the days of imperial persecution could have dreamed of the eighteen weary centuries, during which the saints were yet to wait for their Lord from heaven, they might almost have sat down to flat despair. If Polycarp had foreseen the present state of Asia Minor, or Ignatius that of Syria, or Chrysostom that of Constantinople, or Irenaeus that of France, Athanasius that of Egypt, or Augustine that of Africa, their hands might well have trembled, and their knees waxed faint.

Count up, I say, the dark and painful pages of which there are so many in the annals of Church history. Set down in order the heresies and false doctrines, and apostasies, of which there has been such a rank growth – Arianism, and Romanism, and Socinianism, and Neologianism, and their kindred errors. Place before your mind's eye the centuries of ignorance and superstition before the Reformation, and of coldness and formality since Luther's generation passed away. Count up the crimes which have been perpetrated in the name of Christianity – the massacres, the burnings, the persecutions within the Church, not forgetting the Vallenses, the Albigenses, the Spanish Inquisition, the slaughter of the Huguenots and the fires of Smithfield. Do all this faithfully, and I think you will hardly avoid the conclusion, that it was wise mercy which drew so thick a veil over things to come. Wise mercy shewed the early Christians a light in the distance, but did not tell them how far it was away. Wise mercy pointed out the far off harbour lights, but not the stormy sea between. Wise mercy revealed enough to make them work, and hope, and wait. But wise mercy did not tell all that was yet to be fulfilled before the end.

Who thinks of telling his little children in their early years, every trial, and pain, and misery which they may have to go through before they die? Who thinks of filling their tender ears with the particulars of every bodily disease they may have to endure, and every struggle for success in life in which they may have to engage? Who thinks of harrowing up their young souls by describing every bereavement they may have to submit to, or dilating on every deathbed they may have to watch? We do not do it, because they could not understand our meaning, and could not bear the thought of it if they did. And just so, it seems to me, does the Lord Jesus deal with His people in the apocalyptic vision. He keeps back the full revelation of all the way they must go through till the time when He sees they can bear it. He considers our frame. He teaches and reveals as we are able to bear.

After all, there is no argument in reply to those who object to the study of Revelation so powerful as the simple promise of the Word of God. The predictions of Revelation may seem to many improbable and absurd. The differences and mistakes of interpreters may fill others with disgust and dislike to the very name of apocalyptic study. The acknowledged mysteriousness, and confessed difficulties of the book, may incline many to shrink from perusing it. But there the book stands, part of those Scriptures which are all given by inspiration, and all profitable. And there on the forefront of the book stands a promise and an encouragement to the reader and hearer: *Blessed is he that readeth, and they that hear.* These words, no doubt, were spoken in foresight of the objections that men would raise against the study of the book. Give these words their full weight. Fall back on them when all other arguments fail. They are a reserve which will never give way. God has said it, and will make it good. 'Blessed is he that readeth, and they that hear the words of the prophecy of this book.'

3. The third and last thing which I now wish to consider is *the number of useful lessons which the book of Revelation is calculated to teach.*

I am anxious to impress this point on your attention. I want you to establish it in your mind as a settled thing, that the book of Revelation is an eminently profitable book for every reader of the Bible to study. It is a fountain to which the poorest and most unlearned shall never go in vain.

I say, then, that there are many blessed and comfortable truths scattered up and down, all over the book of Revelation, which are intelligible to the simplest comprehension, and yet full of food for the most spiritual mind. God has mercifully so ordered the composition of the book, that there is hardly a chapter from which a man may not draw some striking and edifying thought. He may be unskilful in the interpretation of visions. He may have not idea of the meaning of seals, or trumpets, or vials, of the two witnesses, of the woman fleeing into the wilderness, of the first or second beasts. But still, if he perseveres in humble, prayerful study of the whole book, he shall find in almost every page verses which shall richly repay his pains. They shall shine out on him like stars in the dark vault of heaven in a moonless night. They shall refresh him like an oasis in the wilderness and make it impossible for him to say, 'All is barren.' They shall sparkle like precious stones on the shore, as he walks by the deep waters of the mysterious book, and make him feel that his journey in search of treasure is not in vain.[10]

Let me select a few examples, in order to show what I mean.

There is much about *the Lord Jesus Christ* in Revelation. There are names and titles and expressions about Him there, which we find nowhere else. There is a new light thrown on His offices, His power, His care for His people. Surely this alone is no small matter. To know Jesus is life eternal.

To abide in Jesus is to be fruitful. If we are indeed born of the Spirit, we can never hear too much about our Saviour, our Shepherd, our High Priest and Physician. If our hearts are right in the sight of God, we can never hear too much about our King. Like snow in summer, and good news from a far country, so are any fresh tidings about Christ.

There is much about the desperate *corruption of human nature* in Revelation. There is evidence on this subject in the Epistles to the Seven Churches, and the repeated accounts of the incorrigibleness and impenitence of the nations of the earth under judgments which we shall all do well to lay to heart. We can never be too well acquainted with our own sinfulness and weakness. The spring of all humility, thankfulness, grateful love to Christ and close walk with God, is real, thorough, scriptural knowledge of the wickedness of our own hearts. None will ever build high who does not begin low. The soul that loves much is the soul that feels its debt is great, and that much has been forgiven.

There is much about *hell* in Revelation. There are many fearful expressions which show its reality, its misery, its eternity, its certainty. How deeply important is it to have clear views on this solemn subject in the present day! A disposition appears in some quarters to shrink from asserting the eternity of punishment. A flood of that miserable heresy, universalism, seems coming upon us. Amiable and well meaning enthusiasts are speaking smooth things about the love of God being lower than hell, and the mercy of God excluding the exercise of all His other attributes of justice and holiness. Tender-hearted women and intellectual men are catching at the theory that, after all, there is hope in the far distance for everybody, and that Satan's old assertion deserves credit, 'Ye shall not surely die.' Oh, reader, beware of this delusion! Be not wise above that which is written. Believe me, it is a great thing to believe in the reality of hell. Study the apocalyptic visions well, and you will find it hard to disbelieve it.

There is much about *heaven* in Revelation. I speak of heaven in the common acceptation of the word. I mean the future abode of the saints and people of God. And I say that no book in God's Word tells us so much about heaven as the Apocalypse. If there was nothing else to be learned from the book beside this, we ought to be most thankful. Where is there a believer in the Lord Jesus who does not frequently think on the world to come and the resurrection state? Who that has lost a dear friend or relative, who died in the Lord, can abstain from meditating on the life of glory, and the place of meeting? Who among the people of God does not frequently reach forward in imagination into that unknown and unvisited abode, and strive to picture to his mind's eye the manner of the place and its employments? It is mysterious, no doubt. But nowhere is the veil so much lifted up as it is in the book of Revelation.

There is much about *the prospects of the Church of Christ* in Revelation. When I speak of the Church, I mean the Church of the elect, the living body of Christ, whose members are all holy. The pages of the Apocalypse show plainly that the triumphs, and rest, and ease, and peace of that Church are not in this world. Its members must make up their minds to battles and fightings, to trial and persecution, to cross and affliction. They must be content to be a little flock, a poor and despised people, until the advent of Christ. Their good things are yet to come. Well would it be for believers if they would learn from Revelation to moderate the expectations from missions, schools and all other ecclesiastical machinery. Then should we not hear as we now often do, of disappointment, and despondency, and depression among true Christians, and especially among ministers. We live in the time when God is taking out a people. These are the days of election, but not of universal conversion. We are yet in the wilderness. The bridegroom is not yet with us. The days of absence, and mourning, and separation are not yet past and gone.

There is much in Revelation to show *the folly of depending entirely on the powers of this world* for the advancement of true religion. There is much to show that believers should not look to kings, and princes, and rich men, and great men, for the bringing in and support of the kingdom of Christ. The times are not yet come when kings shall literally be 'the nursing fathers' of the churches. It is striking to observe how often the Apocalypse speaks of them as the enemies of God's cause and not the friends. We need this lesson here in England. With a settled conviction that the principle of an established church is scriptural and sound, I still feel we need reminding that alliance with the powers that be has its disadvantages as well as its advantages to the visible Church of Christ. It is apt to engender indolence, apathy and formality among professing Christians. I firmly believe that the Church of England would have exerted itself more and done more for the world, if its members had been more familiar with the book of Revelation, and learned from it to expect little from the State.

There is much in Revelation to show the painful *childishness of the vast majority of true Christians* all over the world. Here we are, the greater part of us, scrambling and wrangling about the merest trifles, contending about forms and ceremonies and outward matters of man's devising, as if they were the essentials of Christianity, talking of order, and precedent, and custom, and routine, while millions of heathen are perishing for lack of knowledge and myriads of our countrymen are dying as ignorant as the heathen around our own doors. And all this time the eternal purposes of God are rolling onto fulfilment, the kingdoms of this world are on the brink of dissolution, the day of judgment is at hand, and an hour draws nigh when Episcopacy, Presbyterianism, Congregationalism, Establishments and voluntary Churches, shall be clean swept out of the way, and nothing but grace, faith and heart-holiness shall abide and stand fire. Never, never do I, for one, read the Apocalypse without feeling the excessive littleness of Christians. We are like children busy with our little houses of sand at low water by the seaside. The tide is rising. Our houses will soon be gone. Happy shall we be if we ourselves escape with our lives!

There is much, in the last place, in Revelation to show *the safety of all true believers in Christ*, whatever may come upon the world. Awful as are the woes of which the Apocalypse speaks, there is not a syllable to show that a hair shall fall from the head of any one of God's children. Hid, like Noah, in the ark; plucked, like Lot, from the fiery judgment; withdrawn, like Elijah, from the reach of their enemies; rescued, like Rahab, from the ruin of all around: they, at least, may read the Revelation without being afraid. The book that looks dark and threatening to the world, speaks no terrors to them. Like the wondrous pillar of cloud at Pihahiroth (Exod. 14) it may fill the mind of an ungodly man with gloom, but, like the same cloud, it shall give light by night to the people of God.

Reader, what shall we say to these things? I have mentioned eight things which stand forth plainly and unmistakably in the book of Revelation. There is no mystery about them. They require no deep learning to understand. A humble mind and a prayerful heart will not fail to discover them.

These are the kind of things which we can never know too well. The offices of the Lord Jesus Christ Himself, the corruption of man, the reality of hell, the nature of heaven, the prospects of the Church, the folly of trusting in princes, the childishness of God's people, the safety of believers in the day of wrath – these are the kind of subjects with which we cannot be too familiar. These are the plain lessons which, with all its many difficulties, Revelation will unfold. Verily if these things are engraven deeply on our minds, our reading of the Apocalypse will be blessed indeed!

These are the kind of things which Satan labours hard to keep us from. Well may that old enemy fill men's minds with prejudice against apocalyptic study. Well may he suggest the evil thought, 'It is all mysterious, it is all too deep, we need not read it.' Let us resist him in this matter. Let us cleave to

Revelation more closely every year. Let us never doubt that it is a profitable study for our souls.

It only remains now to conclude this address with three practical remarks:

1. For one thing, let us thank God that *the things needful to salvation are all clear, plain and devoid of mystery to a humble mind*. Whatever difficulties there may be in the visions of the Apocalypse, the most unlearned reader of the Bible shall never miss the way to heaven, if he seeks to find it in a childlike and prayerful spirit.

The guilt, and corruption, and weakness of man is not a hidden thing, like a seal, a trumpet or a vial.

Christ's power and willingness to save, and justification by faith in Him, are not a dark thing, like the number 666.

The absolute necessity of a new birth and a thorough change of heart is not an uncertainty, like the meaning of the two witnesses.

The impossibility of salvation without meetness for heaven is not a mystery, like the interpretation of the vision of the four living creatures.

But, reader, remember while you thank God for this clear teaching in the things essential to salvation, that this very clearness increases your personal responsibility. Take heed, lest an open door being set before you, any of you should fail to enter in by it and be saved.

Hearken, every one into whose hands this address may come, and understand. I give you a plain warning this day. Do not forget it. You may reach heaven without knowing much about the deep things of the Apocalypse, but you will never get there without the saving knowledge of Christ, and a new heart. You must be born again. You must renounce your own righteousness and acknowledge yourself a sinner. You must wash in the fountain of Christ's blood. You must be clothed in the garment of Christ's righteousness. You must take up the cross of Christ and follow Him.

These are the things *absolutely needful*. These are the things without which no man, learned or unlearned, high or low, can ever be saved.

Rest not, rest not till you *know these things by experience*. Without them you may know the whole list of apocalyptic commentaries, be familiar with all that Mede, and Brightman, and Cressener, and Daubuz, and Durham, and Cuninghame, and Woodhouse, and Elliot, and Alford, and Garratt have written on the subject, and yet rise at the last day a lost soul, knowing much intellectually, like the devils, but, like the devils, ruined for ever.

2. For another thing, let me entreat all students of the book of Revelation, *to beware of dogmatism and positveness* in expressing and maintaining their views of the meaning of its more mysterious portions.

Nothing, I firmly believe has brought more discredit on the study of prophecy than the excessive rashness and over-weening confidence with which many of its advocates have asserted the correctness of their own interpretations, and impugned the expositions of others. Too many have written and talked as if they had a special revelation from heaven, and as if it was impossible for any one to maintain a character for common sense if he did not see with their eyes.[11]

Let us all watch our hearts and be on our guard against this spirit. Dogmatism is a great trap which Satan lays in men's way when he cannot prevent them studying the Apocalypse. Let us not fall into it. Let us rather pray for a spirit of modesty and humility in offering our solutions of the deep things of symbolical prediction. Let us allow that we may possibly be wrong, and that others may possibly be right. Believe me, we all need this caution. We are unhappily prone to be most positive when we have least warrant for our assertions, simply because our pride whispers that our credit for discernment is at stake, and that having made statements mainly on the authority of our own judgment, we are specially bound to defend them.

Happy is that student of prophecy who is willing to confess that there are many things of which he is yet ignorant. Happier still, and more uncommon too, is he who is able to use those three hardest words in the English language, 'I was mistaken.'

3. Finally, let all believers take comfort in the thought that *the end to which all things are coming is clear, plain and unmistakable.* There may yet be judgments in store for the world, of which we know nothing. There may be 'distress of nations with perplexity' far exceeding anything we have yet heard of, read or seen. There may be more grievous wars, and famines, and pestilences, and persecutions yet to come.

But the end is sure. Yet a little while and he that shall come, will come, and will not tarry. The kings of the earth may struggle and contend for their own worldly interests; but sooner or later the kingdoms of this world shall become the kingdoms of our God, and of His Christ. There shall be an eternal peace. He shall come and take possession, 'whose right it is'. The dominion and power shall be given to the saints of the Most High, and of the increase of their peace shall be no end.

Oh, that we may all remember this! In patience let us possess our souls, and in every trying time do as Luther did, repeat the 46th Psalm:

God is our refuge and strength, a very present help in trouble.

Therefore will not we fear, though the earth be removed, and though the mountains be carried into the midst of the sea;

Though the waters thereof roar and be troubled, though the mountains shake with the swelling thereof. Selah.

There is a river, the streams whereof shall make glad the city of God, the holy place of tabernacles of the Most High.

God is in the midst of her; she shall not be moved: God shall help her, and that right early.

The heathen raged, the kingdoms were moved: He uttered His voice, the earth melted.

The Lord of hosts is with us; the God of Jacob is our refuge. Selah.

Come behold the works of the Lord, what desolations He hath made in the earth.

He maketh wars to cease unto the end of the earth; He breaketh the bow, and cutteth the spear in sunder; He burneth the chariot in the fire.

Be still, and know that I am God: I will be exalted among the heathen, I will be exalted in the earth.

The Lord of hosts is with us; the God of Jacob is our refuge. Selah.

7

AND SO ALL ISRAEL SHALL BE SAVED

And so all Israel shall be saved: as it is written, There shall come out of Sion the Deliverer, and shall turn away ungodliness from Jacob (Romans 11:26).

This is one of the great unfulfilled prophecies of Scripture. More than eighteen centuries have rolled round since St. Paul wrote these words. During that period many marvellous and unexpected events have taken place. The world has often been convulsed and turned upside down. Empires and kingdoms have risen and fallen. Nations and peoples have decayed and passed away. Visible Churches have disappeared, and their candlestick been removed. But to this hour, St. Paul's prediction awaits its accomplishment. 'All Israel shall be saved' remains yet unfulfilled.

To a plain man, untrammelled by traditional interpretation, the words of this prophecy appear very simple. It is not like the temple which Ezekiel saw in vision: a dark and obscure thing, of which we may say as Daniel said of another vision, 'I heard, but understood not'. It is not presented to us under the veil of emblems, like the seals, trumpets, vials and beasts in Revelation, about which men will probably never be of one mind till the Lord comes, and the wisest commentator can only conjecture. Nothing of the kind! The sentence before us is a simply categorical proposition, and I firmly believe it means exactly what it appears to mean. Let us analyse it.

And so: that means, as Parkhurst says, 'and then, then at length'. It is an expression of time, rather than manner. It is like Acts 7:8 'And so Abraham begat Isaac'; and 1 Thessalonians 4:17: 'And so shall we ever be with the Lord.'

Israel shall be saved: that means the Jewish nation and people. It cannot possibly mean the Gentiles, because they are mentioned in the verse which directly precedes our text, in direct contrast to the Jews. 'Blindness in part is happened to Israel, until the fullness of the Gentiles be come in' (Rom. 11:25).

All Israel: that means the whole people or nation of the Jews. It cannot possibly mean a small elect remnant. In this very chapter the Israelitish nation and the *election* out of Israel are mentioned in contradistinction to one another. 'Israel hath not obtained that which he seeketh for; but the election hath obtained it; and the rest were blinded' (Rom. 11:7).

Shall be saved: that means, shall be redeemed from their present unbelief and have their eyes opened to see and believe the true Messiah, shall be delivered from their low estate and restored to the favour of God, and shall become a holy nation and a blessing to the world.

So much for the interpretation of our text. I shall now proceed to invite the attention of my readers to four points respecting Israel, which every friend of the 'Jews' should endeavour to keep always fresh and green before his mind. Trite and familiar as they may seem to some, they are overlooked and forgotten by others. But I do not hesitate to say that a firm grasp of these four points is the foundation of any real and abiding interest in the Jewish subject and cause.

1. I ask you, then, in the first place to consider *the very peculiar past history* of this Israel, which is one day 'to be saved'.

For the facts of that history I shall simply refer you to the Bible. Whatever modern scepticism may please to say, the story of Israel which that venerable old Book records is as trustworthy as the story of any ancient nation in the world. We have no more warrant for disputing its accuracy than for disputing the accounts of Egypt, Assyria, Persia and Greece, related by Herodotus. On the contrary, there is continually accumulating evidence that the Old Testament memoirs of the Jewish people are thoroughly trustworthy and true.

Israel, then, we find, for nearly fifteen hundred years was more favoured and privileged by God than any nation in the world. David might well say, 'What one nation in the earth is like Thy people Israel, whom God went to redeem for a people to Himself?' (2 Sam. 7:23). It was the only nation in the earth to which God was pleased to reveal Himself. 'To them were committed the oracles of God' (Rom. 3:2). While all other nations were suffered to walk in their own ways, and to live in moral and spiritual darkness, the Jews alone enjoyed an immense amount of light and knowledge. The humblest priest in Solomon's temple was a far better theologian than Homer; Daniel, and Ezra, and Nehemiah knew more about God than Socrates, and Plato, and Pythagoras, and Cicero put together.

The Jews were brought out of Egypt by miraculous interposition, planted in Palestine, one of the choicest corners of the earth, and fenced off and separated from other nations by peculiar customs and ceremonies. They were supplied with a moral law from heaven so perfect, that even to this day nothing can be added to it or taken from it. They were taught to worship God with ceremonial rites and ordinances, which, however burdensome they may seem to us, were admirably adapted to human nature at that early stage of man's history, and calculated to train them for a higher dispensation. They were constantly warned and instructed by prophets, and protected and defended by miracles. In short, if mercies and kindnesses alone could make people good, no nation on earth should have been so good as Israel. While Egypt, and Babylon, and Greece worshipped the works of their own hands, the Jew alone was a worshipper of the one true God.

But Israel, unhappily, we find, were a people always prone to backsliding and falling away from God. Again and again they fell into idolatry and wickedness and forsook the Lord God of their fathers. Again and again they were chastised for their sins and delivered into the hands of the nations around them. Midianites, Philistines, Ammonites, Syrians, Assyrians, Babylonians were rods by which they were repeatedly scourged. From the time of the Judges down to the end of Chronicles, we see a sorrowful record of constantly recurring rebellions against God, and constantly recurring punishments. Never, apparently, was there a nation so stubborn and obstinate, and so ready to forget instruction, so mercifully dealt with, and yet so impenitent and unbelieving.

Finally, we find Israel at the end of fifteen hundred years given up by God to a fearful punishment, and allowed to reap the consequences of their own sins. After repeatedly rejecting God's prophets, they headed up their wickedness by rejecting God's only begotten Son. They refused their true King, the Son of David, and would have no king but Caesar. Then at last the cup of their iniquity was full. Jerusalem was given up to the Romans. The holy and beautiful temple was burned. The Mosiac services were brought to an end. The Jews themselves were deprived of their land and scattered all over the earth.

The whole history is wonderful, peculiar and unlike anything else that is recorded and known by man. Never was a people so peculiarly favoured and so peculiarly punished. Never did any nation at one time rise so high and at another fall so low. Never was there such a depravity of human nature, and the incessant tendency of man to moral and spiritual decay. Those who are fond of telling us in modern times that kindness and love are sufficient regenerate man and keep man good, are always forgetting the mighty lesson that is taught us by the history of the Jews. The corruption of man is a far worse disease than your modern philosophers suppose. Israel was surrounded by mercies and loving kindness: yet Israel fell. Let that never be forgotten.

2. I shall now ask you in the second place to consider the *very peculiar position which Israel as a nation occupies at the present day.*

In handling this point I shall first simply refer to facts which are open to the observation of every intelligent and well-informed man upon earth, whether believer or unbeliever. I will allow such a man to shut up my Bible for a moment, and I will not ask him to listen to texts. I will only appeal to facts, and I challenge him to defy them if he can.

I assert then that the Jews are at this moment a peculiar people, and utterly separate from all other people on the face of the earth. They fulfil the prophecy of Hosea: 'The children of Israel shall bide many days without a king, and without a prince, and without a sacrifice' (Hos. 3:4). For 1800 years they have been scattered over the globe, without a country, without a government, without a capital city, strangers and aliens everywhere, often fiercely persecuted and vilely treated. Yet to this moment they continue a distinct, isolated and separate nation, far more so than any nation on the earth. The wonderful words of that strange prophet Balaam, which God obliged him to speak, are still literally true: 'The people shall dwell alone, and shall not be reckoned among the nations' (Num. 23:9).

Of what nation or people on earth can the like be said? I answer, confidently, none. When Nineveh and Babylon, and Tyre and the hundred-gated Thebes of Egypt, and Susa, and Persepolis, and Carthage and Palmyra were destroyed, what became of their inhabitants and subjects? We can give no answer. No doubt they were carried away captive and dispersed. But where are they now? No man can tell. When Saxons, and Danes, and Normans, and Flemings under the persecution of Alva, and Frenchmen after the edict of Nantes, settled down in our own England, what became of *them?* They were all gradually absorbed into our own population, and have generally lost all their national distinctions, except, perhaps, in some cases their names. But nothing of the sort has ever happened to the Jews; they are still entirely distinct and never absorbed.

Even in matters of comparatively minor importance, there is to this very day an extraordinary serparateness between the Jews and any other family of mankind on the face of the globe. Time seems unable to efface the difference. At the end of eighteen centuries they are a separate people. *Physically*, they are separate. Who does not know the Jewish type of countenance? Even a man like Mr. Lawrence, in his work on physiology, is obliged to admit that 'the Jews exhibit one of the most striking instances of national formation unaltered by the most remarkable changes' (p 467, ed. 3). In *customs and habits* they are separate. The tenacity with which they still keep to their Saturday Sabbath, and the feast of their law, might put Christians to shame. Even in their *political influence* they are strangely separate. The extraordinary financial power which they exercise in all the money markets of the world, enables them to sway the actions of governments to an extent of which few have any conception. In short, if there ever was a people who are distinct, marked, cut off and separate from others, that people is Israel. Though they have dwelt among the Gentiles for eighteen centuries, they are still as distinct from the Gentiles as black is distinct from white, and seem to be as incapable of mixture or absorption as oil is incapable of being absorbed into, or mixed with, water.

Now how shall we account for this extraordinary state of things? How shall we explain the unique and peculiar position which the Jewish people occupies in the world? Why is it that, unlike the Saxons, and Danes, and Normans, and Flemings, and French, this singular race still floats alone, though broken to pieces like a wreck, on the waters of the globe, amidst its 1500 million inhabitants, and after the lapse of 1800 years is neither destroyed, nor crushed, nor evaporated, nor amalgamated, nor lost sight of; but lives to this day as separate and distinct as it was when the arch of Titus was built at Rome?

I have not the least idea how questions like these are answered by those who profess to deny the divine authority of Scripture. In all my reading I never met with an honest attempt to answer them from the unhappy camp of unbelievers. In fact it is my firm conviction that among the many difficulties of infidelity there is hardly any one more really insurmountable than the separate continuance of the Jewish nation. It is a burdensome stone which your modern sceptical writers may affect to despise, but cannot lift or remove out of their way. God has many witnesses to the truth of the Bible, if men would only examine them and listen to their evidence. But you may depend on it there is no witness so unanswerable as one who always keeps standing up, and living, and moving before the eyes of mankind. That witness is the Jew.

The question, however, about the exceptional and peculiar position of the Jewish people is one that never need puzzle anyone who believes the

Bible. Once open that Book and study its contents, and the knot which so completely baffles the sceptic is one which you can easily untie. The inspired volume which you have in your hands supplies a full and complete explanation. Search it with an honest determination to put a literal meaning on its prophetical portions, and to reject traditional interpretation, and the difficulty will vanish away.

I assert that the peculiar position which Israel occupies in the earth is easily explicable in the light of holy Scripture. They are a people reserved and kept separate by God for a grand and special purpose. That purpose is to make them a means of exhibiting to the world in the latter days God's hatred of sin and unbelief, and God's almighty power and almighty compassion. They are kept separate that they may finally be saved, converted and restored to their own land. They are reserved and preserved, in order that God may show in them, as on a platform, to angels and men, how greatly He hates sin, and yet how greatly He can forgive, and how greatly He can convert. Never will that be realised as it will in that day when 'All Israel shall be saved'.

3. I will ask you in the third place to *consider the very peculiar future prospects of Israel.*

The singular condition of the Jews at the present time, we have seen, is most painful and instructive. They are still lying under the just displeasure of God. Because they despised His prophets and rejected His messages, because they 'would not believe the voice of His Scriptures read to them every Sabbath day', because they killed the Prince of life and were His betrayers and murderers, for all these reasons His wrath is come upon them to the uttermost, and for a time they are cast off and rejected. Like Cain they slew their holy Brother, and like Cain they are fugitives and vagabonds on earth, and bear the mark of God's displeasure. The blood of the Messiah whom they murdered is upon them and their children. And their eyes are yet blinded. The veil is still upon their hearts. They stand before the world at this moment, like a beacon at the top of a hill, a perpetual witness that nothing is so offensive to God as unbelief, formalism, self-righteousness and abuse of privileges. Such is their present position. But what are their future prospects? Let us turn once more to the Bible and see.

The history of Israel then has not yet come to an end. There is another wonderful chapter yet to be unfolded to mankind. The Scripture tells us expressly that a time is coming when the position of Israel shall be entirely changed, and they shall be once more restored to the favour of God. For what saith the Scripture which cannot be broken? What is written in that Book of which no prediction shall ever fail?

I read that when the heart of Israel 'shall turn to the Lord, the veil shall be taken away' (2 Cor. 3:16).

I read that a day is coming when God says, 'I will pour upon the house of David, and upon the inhabitants of Jerusalem, the spirit of grace and of supplications: and they shall look upon Me whom they have pierced, and they shall mourn for him, as one mourneth for his only son' (Zech. 12:10).

I read that in that day 'there shall be a fountain opened to the house of David and to the inhabitants of Jerusalem for sin and uncleanness' (Zech. 13:1). I beg you will remember that the primary application of these prophecies of Zechariah belongs literally to the Jews.

I read, furthermore, that God says in Ezekiel to Israel:

I will take you from among the heathen and gather you out of all countries, and will bring you into your own land. Then will I sprinkle clean water upon you, and ye shall be clean: from all your filthiness and from all your idols, will I cleanse you. A new heart also will I give you, and a new spirit will I put within you: and I will take away the stony heart out of your flesh, and I will give you a heart of flesh. And I will put my Spirit within you, and cause you to walk in my statutes, and ye shall keep my judgements, and do them. And ye shall dwell in the land that I gave to your fathers; and ye shall be my people, and I will be your God. I will also save you from all your uncleannesses: and I will call for the corn, and will increase it, and lay no famine upon you. And I will multiply the fruit of the tree, and the increase of the field, that ye shall receive no more reproach of famine among the heathen. Then shall ye remember your own evil ways, and your doings that were not good, and shall loathe yourselves in your own sight for your iniquities and for your abominations. Not for your sakes do I this, saith the Lord God, be it known unto you: be ashamed and confounded for your own ways, O house of Israel. Thus saith the Lord God; in the day that I shall have cleansed you from all your iniquities I will also cause you to dwell in the cities, and the wastes shall be builded. And the desolate land shall be tilled, whereas it lay desolate in the sight of all that passed by. And they shall say, This land that was desolate is become like the garden of Eden; and the waste and desolate and ruined cities are become fenced, and are inhabited. Then the heathen that are left round about you shall know that I the LORD build the ruined places and plant that which was desolate.: I the LORD have spoken it, and I will do it. Thus saith the Lord God; I will yet for this be enquired of by the house of Israel, to do it for them; I will increase them with men like a flock. As the holy flock, as the flock of Jerusalem in her solemn feasts; so shall the waste cities be filled with flocks of men: and they shall know that I am the LORD (Ezek. 36:24-38).

Once more I remind you that this wonderful passage *primarily* belongs to the JEWS. No doubt the Church of Christ may *secondarily* make a spiritual use of it. But let us never forget that the Holy Ghost first caused it to be written concerning Israel.

But time would fail me, if I attempted to quote all the passages of Scripture in which the future history of Israel is revealed. Isaiah, Jeremiah, Ezekiel, Hosea, Joel, Amos, Obadiah, Micah, Zephaniah, Zechariah all declare the same thing. All predict, with more or less particularity, that in the end of this dispensation the Jews are to be restored to their own land and to the favour of God. I lay no claim to infallibility in the interpretation of Scripture in this matter. I am well aware that many excellent Christians cannot see the subject as I do. I can only say, that to my eyes, the future *salvation* of Israel as a people, their *return* to Palestine and their national conversion to God, appear as clearly and plainly revealed as any prophecy in God's Word.

Concerning *the time* when Israel shall finally be saved, I shrink from offering an opinion. No doubt there are many 'signs of the times' which deserve the serious attention of all Christians, and it would be easy to enumerate them. But, after all, we are always bad judges of anything that happens under our own eyes. We are apt to attach an exaggerate importance to it, for the simple reason that we ourselves are affected by it. Let it suffice us to believe that whatever God has said concerning Israel, God *will* do in His own good time. Let us not be hasty to fix dates. Those last words of our Master are very instructive, when the disciple said, 'Wilt Thou at this time restore again the kingdom to Israel?' He answered, 'It is not for you to know the times and seasons, which the Father has put in His own power' (Acts 1:6, 7). To study prophecy is most useful and brings a special blessing. To turn prophets ourselves is not wise, and brings discredit on the cause of Christianity.

Concerning *the manner* in which the complete salvation of Israel shall be effected, we shall do well not to enquire too closely. We must avoid rash speculation and conjecture. If I may venture an opinion, I should say that Scripture seems to point out that Israel will not be restored and converted without an immense amount of affliction, affliction far exceeding that which preceded their deliverance from Egypt. I see much in the words of Daniel: 'There shall be a time of trouble such as never was since there was a nation even to that same time: and at THAT time thy people shall be delivered, every one that shall be found written in the book' (Dan. 12:1).

I believe the words of Zechariah are yet to be fulfilled, 'It shall come to pass, that in all the land, saith the Lord, two parts therein shall be cut off and die; but the third shall be left therein. And I will bring the third part through the fire, and will refine them as silver is refined, and will try them as gold is tried: they shall call on my name, and I will hear them: I will say, It is my people: and they shall say, The LORD is my God (Zech. 13:8, 9).

But I freely confess that these are deep things. Enough for you and me to know that Israel shall be restored to their own land, and shall be converted and saved, without entering too minutely into particulars. Let me close this branch of my subject with the Apostle's words: 'O the depth of the riches both of the wisdom and knowledge of God. How unsearchable are His judgments, and His ways past finding out' (Rom. 11:33).

Only let us grasp firmly the great principle laid down by Jeremiah:

> Fear not thou, O my servant Jacob, and be not dismayed, O Israel: for, behold, I will save thee from afar off, and thy seed from the land of their captivity; and Jacob shall return, and be in rest and at ease and none shall make him afraid. Fear thou not, O Jacob my servant, saith the LORD: for I am with thee; for I will make a full end of all the nations whither I have driven thee: but I will not make a full end of thee, but correct thee in measure; yet will I not leave thee wholly unpunished (Jer. 46:27, 28).

4. I shall now ask you in the fourth and last place to consider *the peculiar debt which Christians owe to Israel*. I shall touch on this branch of my subject briefly, because it is one with which most people are familiar. But it is a branch of such vast importance that I dare not altogether pass over it. It is one about which we all need to be reminded.

That every Christian is a debtor, and under solemn obligation to do good to his fellow men, is one of the great first principles of the gospel. An ignorant formal churchgoer, who never reads his Bible, or prays with his heart, or thinks seriously about his soul, may not understand this. He is apt to say with Cain, 'Am I my brother's keeper?' 'Let every one mind his own business.' But a man who is taught by the Holy Spirit, who feels his sins, and knows his obligation to Christ, and has tasted the comfort of peace with God, such a man will long to do good to others. He will feel for those who are living without God and without Christ. He will say, 'I am a debtor to Greek and Barbarian, to Africa and India, to China and Hindostan. What can I do to save souls and make others partakers of my blessings?'

Now I ask such a man to consider gravely this day, whether he is not under *special* obligations to the Jew. I ask him to remember that there are peculiar reasons why we should care with more than ordinary care for Israel.

1. To whom do we owe *our Bible?* By what hand was that blessed Book written, which is a lamp to so many feet and a lantern to so many paths, that

Book without which we could neither live with comfort nor with comfort die? I answer that every book in the Old and New Testament, unless we except Job, was written by Jews. The pens which the Holy Ghost guided to put down the words which He inspired, were held by Jewish fingers. The hands which were employed to forge this matchless sword of the Spirit were Jewish hands. Every time we take up that wondrous volume, that volume whose nature and existence no infidel can explain away, every time we draw out of it doctrine, correction, reproof, instruction in righteousness, our eyes fall on matter which passed through Jewish minds. The texts which we live upon now, the texts we shall cling to by memory in death, when sight and hearing fail us, the texts which will be a staff in our hand when we go down into the cold river, these texts were first put down in black and white by Jews. Is this nothing?

2. To whom do we *owe the first preaching of the gospel?* Who were the first to go forth into the world, and proclaim to the Gentiles the unsearchable riches of Christ? Again I answer, they were all Jews. The men who first turned the world upside down and deprive heathen temples of their worshippers, and put to silence the philosophers of Greece and Rome, and made kings and rulers tremble on their judgment seats, and made the name of the crucified Jesus of Nazareth more influential than the name of Caesar, they were all children of Israel. They soon passed away. Many of them died for their preaching. The lamp they lighted was taken up by multitudes of converted Gentiles who walked in their steps.

But the fact remains, that the FIRST to begin that blessed work on which the very life of a Church depends at this day, I mean the preaching of the gospel, were all Jews. Where would Europe be at this moment, if it had not been for an invasion of Jewish preachers who obeyed the call, 'Come over and help us'? Surely this also is something.

3. Above all, what shall we say to the great fact that *the woman of whom the Saviour was born, when He condescended to come into the world was a Jewish woman?* When that grand mystery, the incarnation, took place, the mystery which so many slur over and keep back, when the Word was made flesh and dwelt among us, the virgin who miraculously conceived and bare a son, was a virgin of the house of David. No royal family of Assyria, or Persia, or Greece, or Rome was chosen for this honour. That precious blood which was shed on Calvary for our redemption was the blood which flowed from the body of one who was Man in all things like ourselves, sin only excepted, and took a man's nature by being born of an Israelitish woman. The seed of

the woman, be it always remembered, that bruised the serpent's head, the Mediator between God and man, the Almighty Friend of sinners when He 'took on Him the form of a servant, though equal to God', was pleased to take upon Him the form of a Jew. 'He took on Him the seed of Abraham' (Heb. 2:16).

If facts like these do not make up a peculiar claim on Christians, I am greatly mistaken. In the face of the Bible, the preaching of the gospel and the person of Christ, I am bold to say that Christians owe a peculiar debt to Israel. If there is such a thing as gratitude in the world, every Gentile church on earth is under heavy obligation to the Jews.

But how can our debt be paid? That question admits of being answered in two ways.

On the one hand, we may pay our debt *directly*, by using every reasonable effort to bring the gospel to bear on the minds of our Jewish brethren in every part of the globe. No doubt they need to be approached with peculiar wisdom, delicacy and care. They are not to be treated as heathen, but as men who already hold half the truth, who believe the Old Testament like ourselves, although they do not see and receive its full meaning. But all experience proves that there is everything to encourage those who endeavour to lead Israel to the true Messiah, the Christ of God, with love and patience.

Now, as in the Apostles' time, though the nation as a whole remains unbelieving, there is a 'remnant according to the election of grace.' I repeat, there is abundant encouragement to do what the Society of Promoting Christianity among the Jews does and to preach the gospel directly to the Jews. If Saul the Pharisee was converted and made a Christian, I know not why we should despair of the conversion of any Israelite upon earth, in Europe, Asia, Africa or America.

On the other hand, we may all pay our debt *indirectly* by striving to remove stumbling-blocks which now lie between the Jews and Christianity. It is s sorrowful confession to make, but it must be made, that no thing perhaps so hardens Israel in unbelief as the sins and inconsistencies of professing Christians. The name of Christ is too often blasphemed among Jews, by reason of the conduct of many who call themselves Christians. We repel Israel from the door of life, and disgust them by our behaviour. Idolatry among the Roman Catholics, scepticism among Protestants, neglect of the Old Testament, contempt for the doctrine of atonement, shameless Sabbath breaking, widespread immorality, all these things, we may depend on it, have a deep effect on the Jews. They have eyes and they can see. The name of Christ is discredited and dishonoured among them by the practice of those who have been baptised in Christ's name. The more boldly and decidedly all true Christians set their faces against the things I have just named, and wash their hands of any complicity with them, the more likely are they to find their efforts to promote Christianity among the Jews prosperous and successful.

And now let me conclude all with a few plain words of application. I ask all who read this paper to take up the cause of the 'Jews' Society' and the Jewish subject, for the following reasons.

1. Take up the subject because of the *important position which it occupies in Scripture*. Cultivate the habit of reading prophecy with a single eye to the literal meaning of its proper names. Cast aside the old traditional idea that Jacob, and Israel, and Judah, and Jerusalem, and Zion must always mean the Gentile Church, and that predictions about the second Advent are to be taken spiritually, and first Advent predictions literally. Be just, and honest, and fair. If you expect the Jews to take the 53rd of Isaiah literally, be sure you take the 54th, 60th and 62nd literally also. The Protestant Reformers were not perfect. On no point, I venture to say, were they so much in the wrong as in the interpretation of Old Testament prophecy. Even our venerable Authorised Version of the Bible has many 'tables of contents' which are sadly calculated to mislead, in the prophetical books. When the Revised Version comes out, I trust we shall see a great improvement in this respect.

2. In the next place, take up the Jewish subject *because of the times in which we live*. That man must be blind indeed who does not observe how much the attention of politicians and statesmen in these days is concentrating on the countries around Palestine. The strange position of things in Egypt, the formation of the Suez Canal, the occupation of Cyprus, the project of the Euphrates railway, the drying up of the Turkish empire, the trigononmetrical survey of Palestine, what curious phenomena these are! What do they mean? What is going to happen next? He that believeth will not make haste. I will not pretend to decide. But I think I hear the voice of God saying, 'Remember the Jews, look to Jerusalem.'

3. In the next place, take up the Jewish subject *because of the special blessing* which seems to be given to those who care for Israel. I challenge any one to deny that few ministers of Christ have been so useful of late years and made a greater mark on the world than the following well-known men, Charles Simeon, Edward Bickersteth, Haldane Stewart, Dr. Marsh, Robert McCheyne and, though last not least, Hugh McNeile. They were men of very different gifts and minds; but they had one common feature in their religion.

They loved the cause of the Jews. In them was the promise fulfilled. 'They shall prosper that love thee' (Ps. 122:6).

4. In the next place, take up the Jewish subject because of its *close connection with the second Advent of Christ and the close of this dispensation*. Is it not written, 'When the Lord shall build up Zion, He shall appear in His glory' (Ps. 102:16). If the casting away of Israel be the reconciling of the world, what shall the receiving of them be, but life from the dead (Rom. 11:15). The words which the angel Gabriel addressed to the Virgin Mary have never yet been fulfilled: 'He shall reign over the house of Jacob for ever; and of His kingdom there shall be no end' (Luke 1;33).

5. Last of all, let us annually support *that great and good institution, the Jews' Society*, by our money and our prayers. Our money will be well bestowed on an old and faithful servant of Christ, which does Christ's work in Christ's own way. Our prayers are well bestowed if given for a cause which is so near our Master's heart. The time is short. The night of the world is drawing near. If ever there is a 'nation born in a day', that nation will be Israel. Let us pray for that blessed consummation, and give habitually as if we really believed the words, 'All Israel shall be saved.'

8

THE HEIRS OF GOD[12]

As many as are led by the Spirit of God, they are the sons of God. For ye have not received the spirit of bondage again to fear; but ye have received the Spirit of adoption, whereby we cry, Abba, Father. The Spirit itself beareth witness with our spirit, that we are the children of God: And if children, then heirs: heirs of God, and joint heirs with Christ; if so be that we suffer with Him, that we may be also glorified together (Rom. 8:14-17).

The passage of Scripture which heads this page is one which ought to raise within us great searchings of heart. It summons us to consider the solemn question, Am I an heir of God? Am I an heir of glory?

Reader, mark well what I say. I am not speaking of any earthly inheritance. I am not writing of matters which only concern the rich, the great and the noble. I do not ask whether you are an heir to money or lands. I only want you to consider seriously whether you are an heir of God, and an heir of glory?

The inheritance I speak of is the only inheritance *really worth having*. All others are unsatisfying and disappointing. They bring with them many cares. They cannot cure an aching heart. They cannot lighten a heavy conscience. They cannot keep off family troubles. They cannot prevent sicknesses, bereavements, separations and deaths. But there is no disappointment among the heirs of glory.

The inheritance I speak of is the only inheritance *which can be kept for ever*. All others must be left in the hour of death, if they have not been taken away before. The owners of millions of pounds can carry nothing with them beyond the grave. But it is not so with the heirs of glory. Their inheritance is eternal.

The inheritance I speak of is the only inheritance *which is within everybody's grasp*. Most men can never obtain riches and greatness, though they labour hard for them all their lives. But glory, honour and eternal life, are offered to every man freely, who is willing to accept them on God's terms. 'Whosoever will', may be an heir of glory.

Reader, if you wish to have a portion of this inheritance, you must be a member of the one family on earth to which it belongs, and that is the family of all true Christians. You must become one of God's children on earth, if you desire to have glory in heaven. I write to persuade you to become a child of God this day, if you are not one already. I write to persuade you to make sure work that you are one, if at present you have only a vague hope and nothing more. None but true Christians are the children of God. None but the children of God are heirs of glory. Give me your attention, while I try to unfold to you these things, and to show you the lessons which the verses you have already read contain.

1. Let me show you *the relation of all true Christians to God. They are 'sons of God'.*

2. Let me show you *the special evidence of this relation.* True Christians are *led by the Spirit.* They have the *Spirit of adoption.* They have the *witness of the Spirit.* They *suffer with Christ.*

3. Let me show you *the special privileges of this relation.* True Christians are *heirs of God, and joint heirs with Christ.*

1. First, let me show you *the relation of all true Christians to God.* They are God's *sons.*

I know no higher and more comfortable word that could have been chosen. To be servants of God, to be subjects, soldiers, disciples, friends, all these are excellent titles. But to be the sons of God, is a step higher still. What says the Scripture? 'The servant abideth not in the house for ever, but the Son abideth ever' (John 8:35).

To be son of the rich and noble in this world, to be son of the princes and kings of the earth, this is reckoned a privilege. But to be a son of the King of kings, and Lord of lords, to be a son of the High and Holy One, who inhabiteth eternity, this is something higher still. And yet this is the portion of every true Christian.

The son of an earthly parent looks naturally to his father for affection, maintenance, provision and education. There is a home always open to him. There is a love which no bad conduct can completely extinguish. All these are things belonging even to the sonship of this world. Think then how great is the privilege of that poor sinner of mankind, who can say of God, 'He is my Father.'

But HOW can sinful men like you and me become sons of God? When do we enter into this glorious relationship? We are not the sons of God by nature. We are not born so when we come into the world. No man has a natural right to look to God as his Father. It is a vile heresy to say that he has. Men are said to be born poets and painters, but men are never born sons of God. The Epistle to the Ephesians tells us, 'Ye were by nature children of wrath even as others' (Eph. 2:3). The Epistle of St. John says, 'the children of God are manifest, and the children of the devil: whosoever doeth not righteousness is not of God' (1 John 3:10). The Cathechism of the Church of England wisely follows the doctrine of the Bible, and teaches us to say, 'We are by nature born in sin, and children of wrath'. Yes we are rather children of the devil than children of God! Sin is indeed hereditary, and runs in the family of Adam. Grace is anything but hereditary, I and holy men have not, as a matter of course, holy sons. How then and when does this mighty change and translation come upon men? When and in what manner do sinners become sons and daughters of the Lord Almighty?

Men become sons of God in the day that the Spirit leads them to believe on Jesus Christ for salvation, and not before.[13] What says the Epistle to the Galatians? 'Ye are all the children of God by faith in Christ Jesus' (Gal. 3:26). What says the Epistle to the Corinthians? 'Of him are ye in Christ Jesus' (1 Cor. 1:30). What says the Gospel of John? 'As many as received Christ, to them gave He power (or privilege) to become the sons of God, even to them that believe on His name' (John 1:12). Faith unites the sinner to the Son of God, and makes him one of His members. Faith makes him one of those in whom the Father sees no spot, and is well-pleased. Faith marries him to the beloved Son of God, and entitles him to be reckoned among the sons. Faith gives him fellowship with the Father and the Son. Faith grafts him into the Father's family, and opens up to him a room in the Father's house. Faith gives him life instead of death, and makes him instead of being a servant a son. Show me a man that has this faith, and whatever be his church, or denomination, I say that he is a son of God.

Reader, this is one of those points you should never forget. You and I know nothing of a man's sonship *until he believes*. No doubt the sons of God are foreknown and chosen from all eternity, and predestinated to adoption. But, remember, it is not till they are called in due time, and believe, it is not till then that you and I can be certain they are sons. It is not till they repent and believe, that the angels of God rejoice over them. The angels cannot read the book of God's election. They know not who are His 'hidden ones' in the earth. They rejoice over no man till he believes. But when they see some poor sinner repenting and believing, then there is joy among them, joy that one more brand is plucked from the burning, and one more son and heir born again to the Father in heaven. But once more I say, you and I know nothing certain about a man's sonship to God, *until he believes on Christ.*

I solemnly warn every one to beware of the delusive notion, that all men and women are alike children of God, whether they have faith in Christ or not. It is a wild theory which many are clinging to in these days, but one which cannot be proved out of the Word of God. It is a perilous dream, with which many are trying to soothe themselves, but one from which there will be a fearful waking up at the last day.

That God in a certain sense is the universal Father of all mankind, I do not pretend to deny. He is the Great First Cause of all things. He is the Creator of all mankind, and in Him alone, all men, whether Christians or heathens, 'live and move and have their being'. All this is unquestionably true. In this sense Paul told the Athenians, a poet of their own had truly said, *'we are His offspring'* (Acts 17:28). But this sonship gives no man a title to heaven. The sonship which we have by creation is one which belongs to stones, trees, beasts or even to the devils, as much as to us.

That God loves all mankind with a love of pity and compassion I do not deny. 'His tender mercies are over all his works.' He is 'not willing that any should perish, but that all should come to repentance'. He 'has no pleasure in the death of him that dieth'. All this I admit to the full. In this sense our Lord Jesus tells us, 'God so loved the world that He gave His only begotten Son, that whosoever believeth in Him should not perish, but have eternal life' (John 3:16).

But that God is a reconciled and pardoning Father to any but the members of His Son Jesus Christ, and that they are members of Jesus Christ who do not believe on Him for salvation, this is a doctrine which I utterly deny. The holiness and justice of God are both against the doctrine. They make it impossible for sinful men to approach God, excepting through a mediator. They tell us that God out of Christ is a consuming fire. The whole system of the New Testament is against the doctrine. That system teaches that no man can claim interest in Christ, unless he will receive Him as his Mediator, and believe on Him as his Saviour. Where there is no faith in Christ, it is drivelling folly to say that a man may take comfort in God as his Father. God is a reconciled Father to none but the members of Christ!

It is nonsense to talk of the view I am now upholding as narrow-minded and harsh. The gospel sets an open door before every man. Its promises are wide and full. Its invitations are earnest and tender. Its requirements are simple and clear. 'Only believe on the Lord Jesus Christ, and, whosoever thou art, thou shalt be saved.' But to say that proud men, who will not bow their necks to the easy yoke of Christ, and worldly men, who are determined to have their own way and their sins, to say that such men have a right to claim an interest in Christ, and a right to call themselves sons of God, is absurdity indeed. God offers to be their Father; but He does it on certain distinct terms: they must draw near to Him through Christ. Christ offers to be their Saviour; but in doing it He makes one simple requirement: they must commit their souls to Him, and give Him their hearts. They refuse the terms, and yet dare to call God their Father! They scorn the requirement, and yet dare to hope that Christ will save them! God is to be their Father, but on their own terms! Christ is to be their Saviour, but on their own conditions! What can be more unreasonable? What can be more proud? What can be more unholy than such a doctrine as this? Beware of it, reader, for it is a common doctrine in these latter days. Beware of it, for it is often speciously put forward, and sounds beautiful and charitable in the mouths of poets, novelists, sentimentalists and tender-hearted women. Beware of it, unless you mean to throw aside your Bible altogether and set up yourself to be wiser than God. Stand fast on the old scriptural ground: *no sonship to God without Christ! No interest in Christ without faith!*

I would to God there was not so much cause for giving warnings of this kind. I have reason to think they need to be given clearly and unmistakably. There is a school of theology rising up in this day, which appears to me most eminently calculated to promote infidelity, to help the devil and to ruin souls. It comes to us, like Joab to Amasa, with the highest professions of charity, liberality and love. God is all mercy and love, according to this theology. His holiness and justice are completely left out of sight! Hell is never spoken of in this theology: its talk is all of heaven! Damnation is never mentioned: it is treated as an impossible thing, all men and women are to be saved! Everybody who believes anything has faith! Everybody who thinks anything has the Spirit! Everybody is right! Nobody is wrong! Nobody is to blame for any action he may commit! It is the result of his position! It is the effect of circumstances! He is not accountable for his opinions, any more than for the colour of his skin! He must be what he is! The Bible of course is a very imperfect book! It is old fashioned! It is obsolete! We may believe just as much of it as we please, and no more! Reader, of all this theology I warn you solemnly to beware. In spite of big swelling words about 'liberality' and 'charity' and 'broad views' and 'new lights' and 'freedom from bigotry' and so forth, I do believe it to be a theology that leads to hell rather than to heaven.

Facts are directly against the teachers of this theology. Let them walk round the wards of hospitals, and note the many diseases which rack man's frame. Let them go to the shores of the Dead Sea, and look down into its mysterious bitter waters. Let them observe the wandering Jews, scattered over the face of the world. And then let them tell us, if they dare, that God is so entirely a God of mercy and love, that He never does, and never will, punish sin.

The *conscience of man* is directly against these teachers. Let them go to the bedside of some dying child of the world, and try to comfort him with their doctrines. Let them see if their vaunted theories will calm his gnawing restless anxiety about the future, and enable him to depart in peace. Let them show us, if they can, a few well authenticated cases of joy and happiness in death without Bible promises, without conversion and without that faith in the blood of Christ, which old-fashioned theology enjoins. Alas! when men are leaving the world, conscience makes sad work of these new systems. Conscience is not easily satisfied in a dying hour that there is no such thing as hell.

Every reasonable conception that we can form of a future state is directly against these teachers. Fancy a heaven which should contain all mankind! Fancy a heaven in which holy and unholy, pure and impure, good and bad, would be all gathered together in one confused mass! What point of union would there be in such a company? What common bond of harmony and brotherhood? What common delight in a common service? What concord, what harmony, what peace, what oneness of spirit could exist? Surely the mind revolts from the idea of a heaven in which there would be no distinction between the righteous and the wicked, between Pharaoh and Moses, between Abraham and the Sodomites, between Paul and Nero, between Peter and Judas Iscariot, between the man who dies in the act of murder or drunkenness and men like Baxter, Wilberforce and M'Cheyne! Surely an eternity in such a miserably confused crowd would be worse than annihilation itself! Surely such a heaven would be no better than hell!

The *interests of all holiness and morality* are directly against these teachers. If all men and women alike are God's children, whatever is the difference between them in their lives – and all alike going to heaven, however different they may be from one another here in this world – where is the use of labouring after holiness at all? What motive remains for 'living soberly, righteously, and godly'? What does it matter how men conduct themselves, if all go to heaven, and nobody goes to hell? Surely the very heathen of Greece and Rome could tell us something better and wiser than this! Surely a doctrine which is subversive of holiness and morality, and takes away all motives to exertion, carries on the face of it the stamp of its origin. It is of earth, and not of heaven. It is of the devil, and not of God.

The Bible is against these teachers from beginning to end. Hundreds of texts might be quoted which are diametrically opposed to their theories. These texts must be rejected summarily, if the Bible is to square with their views. There may be no valid reason why they should be rejected; but to suit the theology I speak of, they must be thrown away. At this rate the authority of the whole Bible is soon at an end. And what do they give us in place of God's Word, when they have taken it out of our hands? Nothing, nothing at all! They rob us of the bread of life, and do not give us in its stead so much as a stone.

Reader, once more I warn you to beware of this theology. I charge you to hold fast the doctrine which I have been endeavouring to uphold in this address. Remember what I have said, and never let it go. No inheritance of glory without sonship to God! No sonship to God without an interest in Christ! No interest in Christ without your own personal faith! This is God's truth. Never forsake it.

Who now among the readers of this address, *desires to know whether he is a son of God?* Ask yourself this day, and ask it as in God's sight, whether you have repented and believed. Ask yourself whether you are experimentally acquainted with Christ, and united to Him in heart. If not, you may be very sure you are no son of God. you are not yet born again. You are yet in your sins. Your Father in creation God may be, but your reconciled and pardoning Father God is not. Yes! though church and world may agree to tell you to the contrary, though clergy and laity unite in flattering you, your sonship is worth little or nothing in the sight of God. Let God be true and every man a liar. Without faith in Christ you are no son of God, you are not born again.

Who is there among the readers of this address, *who desires to become a son of God?* Let that person see his sins, and flee to Christ for salvation, and this day he shall be placed among the children. Only acknowledge thine iniquity, and lay hold on the hand that Jesus holds out to thee this day, and sonship, with all its privileges, is thine own. Only confess thy sins, and bring them unto Christ, and 'God is faithful and just to forgive thee thy sins, and cleanse thee from all unrighteousness'. This very day old things shall pass away, and all things become new. This very day thou shalt be forgiven, pardoned, accepted in the beloved. This very day thou shalt have a new name given to thee in heaven. Thou didst take up this address a child of wrath. Thou shalt lie down tonight a child of God. Mark this, if thy professed desire after sonship is sincere, if thou art truly weary of thy sins, and hast really something more than a lazy wish to be free, there is real comfort for thee. It is all true. It is all written in Scripture, even as I have put it down. I dare not raise barriers between thee and God. This day I say, 'Believe on the lord Jesus Christ, and thou shalt be a son, and be saved.'

Who is there among the readers of this address that *is a son of God indeed?* Rejoice, I say, and be exceedingly glad of your privileges. Rejoice, for you have good cause to be thankful. Remember the words of the beloved Apostle: 'Behold what manner of love the Father hath bestowed upon us, that we should be called the sons of God' (1 John 3:1). How wonderful that heaven should look down on earth, that the holy God should set His affections on sinful man, and admit him into His family! What though the world does not understand you! What though the men of this world laugh at you, and cast your name as evil! Let them laugh if they will. God is your Father. You have no need to be ashamed. The Queen can create a nobleman. The bishops can ordain clergymen. But Queen, Lords, and Commons, bishops, priests, and deacons, all together cannot, of their own power, make one son of God, or one of greater dignity than a son of God. The man that can call God his Father, and Christ his elder Brother, that man may be poor and lowly, yet he never need be ashamed.

2. Let me show you, in the second place, *the special evidences of the true Christian's relation to God.*

How shall a man make sure work of his sonship? How shall he find out whether he is one that has come to Christ by faith and been born again? What are the marks, and signs, and tokens, by which the sons of God may be known? This is a question which all who love eternal life ought to ask. This is a question to which the verses of Scripture I am asking you to consider, like many others, supply an answer.

i. The sons of God, for one thing, are all *led by His Spirit*. What says the Scripture? 'As many as are led by the Spirit of God, they are the sons of God' (Rom. 8:14).

They are all under the leading and teaching of a power which is almighty, though unseen, even the power of the Holy Ghost. They no longer turn every man to his own way, and walk every man in the light of his own eyes, and follow every man his own natural heart's desire. The Spirit leads them. The Spirit guides them. There is a movement in their hearts, lives and affections, which they feel, though they may not be able to explain, and a movement which is always more or less in the same direction.

They are led away from sin, away from self-righteousness, away from the world. This is the road by which the Spirit leads God's children. Those whom God adopts he teaches and trains. He shows them their own hearts. He makes them weary of their own ways. He makes them long for inward peace.

They are led to Christ. They are led to the Bible. They are led to prayer. They are led to holiness. This is the beaten path along which the Spirit makes them to travel. Those whom God adopts He always sanctifies. He makes sin very bitter to them. He makes holiness very sweet.

It is the Spirit who leads them to Sinai, and first shows them the law, that their hearts may be broken. It is He who leads them to Calvary, and shows them the cross, that their hearts may be bound up and healed. It is He who leads them to Pisgah, and gives them distant views of the promised land, that their hearts may be cheered. When they are taken into the wilderness, and taught to see their own emptiness, it is the leading of the Spirit. When they are carried up to Tabor, and lifted up with glimpses of the glory to come, it is the leading of the spirit. Each and all of God's sons is the subject of these leadings. Each and all yields himself willingly to them. And each and all is led by the right way, to bring him to a city of habitation.

Reader, settle this down in your heart, and do not let it go. The sons of God are a people led by the Spirit of God, and always led more or less in the same way. Their experience will tally wonderfully when they compare notes in heaven. This is one mark of sonship.

ii. Furthermore, all the sons of God *have the feelings of adopted children towards their Father in heaven*. What says the Scripture? 'Ye have not received the Spirit of bondage again to fear, but ye have received the Spirit of adoption, whereby we cry, Abba, Father' (Rom. 8:15).

The sons of God are delivered from that slavish fear of God, which sin begets in the natural heart. They are redeemed from that feeling of guilt, which made Adam hide himself in the trees of the garden, and Cain go out from the presence of the Lord. They are no longer afraid of God's holiness, and justice, and majesty. They no longer feel as if there was a great gulf and barrier between themselves and God, and as if God was angry with them, and must be angry with them, because of their sins. From these chains and fetters of the soul, the sons of God are delivered.

Their feelings towards God are now those of peace and confidence. They see Him as a Father reconciled in Christ Jesus. They look on Him as a God whose attributes are all satisfied by their great Mediator and Peacemaker, the Lord Jesus, as a God who is just, and yet the Justifier of every one that believeth on Jesus. As a Father, they draw near to Him with boldness. As a Father, they can speak to Him with freedom. They have exchanged the spirit of bondage for that of liberty, and the spirit of fear for that of love. They know that God is holy, but they are not afraid. They know that they are sinners, but they are not afraid. Though God is holy, they believe that He is completely reconciled. Though they are sinners, they believe they are clothed all over with Jesus Christ. Such is the feeling of the sons of God.

I allow that some of them have this feeling more vividly than others. Some of them carry about scraps and remnants of the old spirit of bondage to their dying day. Many of them have fits and paroxysms of the old man's complaint of fear returning upon them at intervals. But very few of the sons of God could be found who would not say, if cross-examined, that since they knew Christ they have had very different feelings towards God, from what they ever had before. They feel as if something like the old Roman form of adoption had taken place between themselves and their Father in heaven. They feel as if He had said to each one of them, 'Wilt thou be my son?' and as if their hearts had replied, 'I will.'

Reader, try to grasp this also, and hold it fast. The sons of God are a people who feel towards God in a way that the children of the world do not. They fel no more slavish fear towards Him. They fel towards Him as a reconciled parent. This, then, is another mark of sonship.

iii. But again, the sons of God *have the witness of the Spirit in their consciences*. What says the Scripture? 'The Spirit itself beareth witness with our spirit, that we are the children of God' (Rom. 8:16).

They have all got something within their hearts, which tells them there is a relationship between themselves and God. They feel something which tells them that old things are passed away, and all things become new, that guilt is gone, that peace is restored, that heaven's door is open, and hell's door is shut. They have, in short, what the children of the world have not, a felt, positive, reasonable hope. They have what Paul calls the 'seal' and 'earnest' of the Spirit (2 Cor. 1:22; Eph. 1:13).

Reader, I do not for a moment deny that this witness of the Spirit is exceedingly various in the extent to which the sons of God possess it. With

156

some it is a loud, clear, ringing, distinct testimony of conscience: 'I am Christ's and Christ is mine.' With others it is a little, feeble, stammering whisper, which the devil and the flesh often prevent being heard. Some of the children of God speed on their course towards heaven under the full sails of assurance. Others are tossed to and fro all their voyage, and will scarce believe they have got faith.

But take the least and lowest of the sons of God. Ask him if he will give up the little bit of religious hope which he has attained? Ask him if he will exchange his heart, with all its doubts and conflicts, its fightings and fears, ask him if he will exchange that heart for the heart of the downright worldly and careless man? Ask him if he would be content to turn round and throw down the things he has got hold of, and go back to the world? Who can doubt what the answer would be? 'I cannot do that,' he would reply: 'I do not know whether I have faith: I do not feel sure I have got grace; but I have got something within me I would not like to part with.' And what is that 'something'? I will tell you. It is the witness of the Spirit.

Reader, try to understand this also. The sons of God have the 'witness of the Spirit' in their consciences. This is another mark of sonship.

iv. One thing more let me add. All the sons of God *take part in suffering with Christ*. What says the Scripture? 'If children, then heirs, heirs of God and joint heirs with Christ, if so be that we suffer with Him' (Rom. 8:17).

All the children of God have a cross to carry. They have trials, troubles and afflictions to go through for the gospel's sake. They have trials from the world, trials from the flesh and trials from the devil. They have trials of feeling from relations and friends, hard words, hard conduct and hard judgment. They have trials in the matter of character: slander, misrepresentation, mockery, insinuation of false motives, all these often rain thick upon them. They have trials in the matter of worldly interest. They have often to choose whether they will please man and lose glory, or gain glory and offend man. They have trials from their own hearts. They have each generally their own thorn in the flesh, their own home-devil, who is their worst foe. This is the experience of the sons of God.

Some of them suffer more and some less. Some of them suffer in one way and some in another. God measures out their portions like a wise physician, and cannot err. But never, I believe, was there one child of God who reached Paradise without a cross.

Suffering is the diet of the Lord's family. 'Whom the Lord loveth He chasteneth.' 'If ye be without chastisement, then are ye bastards and not sons.' 'Through much tribulation we must enter the kingdom of God.' When Bishop Latimer was told by his landlord that he had never had a trouble, ' Then,' said he, 'God cannot be here.'

Suffering is a part of the process by which the sons of God are sanctified. They are chastened to wean them from the world, and to make them partakers of God's holiness. The Captain of their salvation was made perfect through sufferings, and so are they. There never yet was a great saint who had not either great afflictions or great corruptions. Well said Philip Melanchthon, 'Where there are no cares, there will generally be no prayers.'

Reader, try to settle this down into your heart also. The sons of God have all to bear a cross. A suffering Saviour generally has suffering disciples. The Bridegroom of the Church was 'a man of sorrows'. The bride must not be a woman of pleasures, and unacquainted with grief. Blessed are they that mourn! Let us not murmur at the cross. This is also a sign of sonship. No cross, no crown!

Reader, I warn you never to suppose that you are a son of God except you have the scriptural marks of sonship. Beware of a sonship without evidences. Again I say, beware. When a man has no leading of the Spirit to show me, no spirit of adoption to tell of, no witness of the Spirit in his conscience, no cross in his experience, is this man a son of God? God forbid that I should say so! His spot is not the spot of God's children. He is no heir of glory.

Tell me not that you have been baptised, and taught the Catechism of the Church of England, and therefore must be a child of God. I tell you that the parish register is not the book of life. I tell you that to be styled a child of God, and called regenerate in infancy by the faith and charity of the prayer book, is one thing; but to be a child of God in deed is another thing altogether. Go and read that Catechism again. It is the 'death unto sin and the new birth unto righteousness' which makes men *children of grace*. Except you know these by experience you are no son of God.

Tell me not that you are a member of Christ's Church, and so must be a son. I answer that the sons of the Church are not necessarily the sons of God. Such sonship is not the sonship of the 8th of Romans. That is the sonship you must have, if you are to be saved.

And now, I doubt not, some reader of this address will want to know if he may not be saved without the witness of the Spirit.

I answer, if you mean by the witness of the Spirit, the full assurance of hope, you may be so saved without question.

But if you want to know whether a man can be saved without any inward sense or knowledge, or hope of salvation, I answer that ordinarily he cannot.

I warn you plainly to cast away all indecision as to your state before God, and to make your calling sure. Clear up your position and relationship. Do not think there is anything praiseworthy in always doubting. Leave that to the Papist. Do not fancy it wise to be ever living like the borderers of old time, on the 'debatable ground'.

'Assurance,' said old Dod, the Puritan, 'may be attained: and what have we been doing all our lives since we became Christians if we have not yet attained it?'

I doubt not some true Christians who read this address will think their evidence of sonship is too small to be good, and will write bitter things against themselves. Let me try to cheer them. Who gave you the feelings you possess? Who made you hate sin? Who made you love Christ? Who made you long and labour to be holy? Whence did these feelings come? Did they come from nature? There are no such products in the natural man's heart. Did they come from the devil? He would fain stifle such feelings altogether. Cheer up and take courage. Fear not, neither be cast down. Press forward, and go on. There is hope for you after all. Strive. Labour. Seek. Ask. Knock. Follow on. You shall yet see that you are sons of God.

3. Let me show you, in the last place, *the privileges of the true Christian's relation to God.*

Nothing can be conceived more glorious than the prospects of the sons of God. The words of Scripture which head this address contain a rich mine of good and comfortable things. 'If we are children,' says Paul, 'we are heirs, heirs of God, and joint heirs with Christ, to be glorified together with Him' (Rom. 8:17).

True Christians then are 'heirs'. Something is prepared for them all which is yet to be revealed.

They are 'heirs of God'. To be heirs of the rich on earth is something. How much more then is it to be a son and heir of the King of kings!

They are 'joint heirs with Christ'. They shall share in His majesty and take part in His glory. They shall be glorified together with Him.

And this, remember, is for all the children. Abraham took care to provide for all his children, and God takes care to provide for His. None of them are disinherited. None will be cast out. None will be cut off. Each shall stand in his lot, and have a portion, in the day when the Lord brings many sons to glory.

Reader, who can tell the full nature of the inheritance of the saints in light? Who can describe the glory which is yet to be revealed and given to the children of God? Words fail us. Language falls short. Mind cannot conceive fully, and tongue cannot express perfectly, the things which are comprised in the glory yet to come upon the sons and daughters of the Lord Almighty. Oh, it is indeed a true saying of the Apostle John! 'It doth not yet appear what we shall be' (1 John 3:2).

The very Bible itself only lifts the veil a little which hangs over this subject. How could it do more? We could not thoroughly understand more if more had been told us. Our frame of mind is as yet too earthly, our understanding is as yet too carnal to appreciate more, if we had it. The Bible generally deals with the subject in negative terms, and not in positive assertions. It describes what there will not be in the glorious inheritance, that thus we may get some faint idea of what there will be. It paints the *absence* of certain things, in order that we may drink in a little of the blessedness of the things *present*. It tells us that the inheritance is 'incorruptible, undefiled, and fadeth not away'. It tells us that the crown of glory 'fadeth not away'. It tells us that the devil is to be bound, that there shall be no more night and no more curse, that death shall be cast into the lake of fire, that all tears shall be wiped away and that the inhabitant shall no more say 'I am sick'. And these are glorious things indeed! No corruption! No fading! No withering! No devil! No curse of sin! No sorrow! No tears! No sickness! No death! Surely the cup of the children of God will indeed run over!

But, reader, there are positive things told us about the glory yet to come upon the heirs of God, which ought not to be kept back. There are many sweet, pleasant and unspeakable comforts in their future inheritance, which all true Christians would do well to consider. There are cordials for fainting pilgrims in many words and expressions of Scripture, which you and I ought to lay up against time of need.

Is *knowledge* pleasant to us now? Is the little that we know of God, and Christ, and the Bible, precious to our souls, and do we long for more? We shall have it perfectly in glory. What says the Scripture? 'Then shall I know even as also I am known' (1 Cor. 13:12). Blessed be God, in heaven there will be no more disagreements among believers! Episcopalians and Presbyterians, Calvinists and Arminians, Millenarians and Antimillenarians, friends of Establishments and friends of the voluntary system, advocates of infant baptism and advocates of adult baptism, all will at length see eye to eye. The former ignorance will have passed away. We shall marvel to find how childish and blind we have been.

Is *holiness* pleasant to us now? Is sin the burden and bitterness of our lives? Do we long for entire conformity to the image of God? We shall have it perfectly in glory. What says the Scripture? 'Christ gave Himself for the Church, that He might present it to Himself a glorious Church, not having spot or wrinkle, or any such thing' (Eph. 5:27). Oh, the blessedness of an eternal goodbye to sin! Oh, how little the best of us do at present! Oh, what unutterable corruption sticks, like bird lime, to all our motives, all our thoughts, all our words, all our actions? Oh, how many of us, like Naphtali, are goodly in our words, but like Reuben, unstable in our works! Thank God, all this shall be changed!

Is *rest* pleasant to us now? Do we often feel faint though pursuing? Do we long for a world in which we need not to be always watching and warring? We shall have it perfectly in glory. What saith the Scripture? 'There remaineth a rest for the people of God' (Heb. 4:9). The daily, hourly conflict with the world, the flesh and the devil, shall at length be at an end. The enemy shall be bound. The warfare shall be over. The wicked shall at last cease from troubling. The weary shall at length be at rest. There shall be a great calm.

Is *service* pleasant to us now? Do we find it sweet to work for Christ, and yet groan, being burdened by a feeble body? Is our spirit often willing, but hampered and clogged by the poor weak flesh? Have our hearts burned within us, when we have been allowed to give a cup of cold water for Christ's sake, and have we sighed to think what unprofitable servants we are? Let us take comfort. We shall be able to serve perfectly, and without weariness, in glory. What saith the Scripture? 'They serve Him day and night in His temple' (Rev. 7:15).

Is *satisfaction* pleasant to us now? Do we find the world empty? Do we long for the filling up of every void place and gap in our hearts? We shall have it perfectly in glory. We shall no longer have to mourn over cracks in all our earthen vessels, and thorns in all our roses, and bitter dregs in all our sweet cups. We shall no longer lament with Jonah over withered gourds. We shall no longer say with Solomon, 'all is vanity and vexation of spirit'. We shall no longer cry with aged David, 'I have seen an end of all perfection'. What saith the Scriptures? 'I shall be satisfied when I awake with Thy likeness' (Ps. 17:15).

Is *communion with the saints* pleasant to us now? Do we feel that we are never so happy as when we are with the excellent of the earth? Are we never so much at home as in their company? We shall have it perfectly in glory. What saith the Scripture? 'The Son of man shall send His angels, and they shall gather out of His kingdom all things that offend, and them which work iniquity.' 'He shall send His angels with a great sound of a trumpet, and they shall gather together His elect from the four winds' (Matt. 13:41; 24:31). Praised be God! We shall see all the saints of whom we have read in the Bible, and in whose steps we have tried to walk. We shall see apostles, prophets, patriarchs, martyrs, reformers, missionaries and ministers, of whom the world was not worthy. We shall see the faces of those we have known and loved in Christ on earth, and over whose departure we shed bitter tears. We shall see them more bright and glorious than ever they were before. And best of all, we shall see them without hurry and anxiety, and without feeling that we only meet to part again. In glory there is no death, no parting, no farewell!

Is *communion with Christ* pleasant to us now? Do we find His name precious to us? Do we feel our hearts burn within us at the thought of His dying love? We shall have perfect communion with Him in glory. 'We shall ever be with the Lord' (1 Thess. 4:17). We shall be with Him in Paradise. We shall see His face in the kingdom. These eyes of ours will behold those hands and feet which were pierced with nails, and that head which was crowned with thorns. Where He is, there will the sons of God be. When He comes, they will come with Him. When He sits down in His glory, they shall sit down by His side. Blessed prospect indeed! I am a dying man in a dying world! All before me is dark! The world to come is a harbour unknown! But Christ is there and that is enough. Surely if there is rest and peace in following Him by faith on earth, there will be far more rest and peace when we see Him face to face. If we have found it good to follow the pillar of cloud and fire in the wilderness, we shall find it a thousand times better to sit down in our eternal inheritance with our Joshua in the promised land.

Ah! reader, if you are not yet among the sons and heirs, I do pity you with all my heart. How much you are missing! How little true comfort you are enjoying! There you are, struggling on, and toiling in the fire, and wearying yourself for mere earthly ends; seeking rest and finding none, chasing shadows and never catching them; wondering *why* you are not happy, and yet refusing to see the cause; hungry, and thirsty, and empty, and yet blind to the plenty within your reach. Oh, that you were wise! Oh, that you would hear the voice of Jesus and learn of Him!

Reader, if you are one of those who are sons and heirs, you may well rejoice and be happy. You may well wait like the boy Patience in *Pilgrim's Progress.* Your best things are yet to come. You may well bear crosses without murmuring. Your light affliction is but for a moment. The sufferings of this present time are not worthy to be compared to the glory which is to be revealed. When Christ our life appears, then you also shall appear with Him in glory. You may well not envy the transgressor and his prosperity. You are the truly rich. Well said a dying believer in my own parish, 'I am more rich than I ever was in my life.' You may say as Mephibosheth said to David, 'Let the world take all, my King is coming again in peace.' You may say as Alexander said when he gave all his riches away and was asked what he kept for himself: 'I have hope.' You may well not be cast down by sickness. The eternal part of you is safe and provided for, whatever happens to your body. You may well look calmly on death. It opens a door between you and your inheritance. You may well not sorrow excessively over the things of the world, over partings and bereavements, over losses and crosses. The day of gathering is before you. Your treasure is beyond reach of harm. Heaven is becoming every year more full of those you love, and earth more empty. Glory in your inheritance! It is all yours if you are a son of God. 'If we are children, then we are heirs.'

1. And now, reader, in concluding this address, *let me ask you, 'Whose child are you?'* Are you the child of nature or the child of grace? Are you the child of the devil or the child of God? You cannot be both at once. Which are you?

Settle the question, reader, for you must die at last either one or the other. Settle it, reader, for it can be settled, and it is folly to leave it doubtful. Settle it, for time is short, the world is getting old, and you are fast drawing near to the judgment seat of Christ. Settle it for death is nigh, the Lord is at hand, and who can tell what a day might bring forth? Oh, that you would never rest till the question is settled! Oh, that you may never feel satisfied till you can say 'I have been born again; I am a son of God'.

2. Reader, *if you are not a son and heir of God, let me entreat you to become one without delay.* Would you be rich? There are unsearchable riches in Christ. Would you be noble? Believing in Christ, you shall be a king. Would you be happy? You shall have a peace which passeth understanding, and which the world can never give, and never take away. Oh, come out, and take up the cross, and follow Christ! Come out from among the thoughtless and worldly, and hear the word of the Lord: 'I will receive you, and will be a Father unto you, and ye shall be my sons and daughters, saith the Lord Almighty' (2 Cor. 6:18).

3. Reader, *if you are a son of God, I beseech you to walk worthy of your Father's house. I* charge you solemnly to honour Him in your life, and above all to honour Him by implicit obedience to all His commands, and hearty love to all His children. Labour to travel through the world like a child of God and

heir of glory. Let men be able to trace a family likeness between you and Him that begat you. Live a heavenly life. Seek things that are above. Do not seem to be building your nest below. Behave like a man who seeks a city out of sight, whose citizenship is heaven and who is willing to put up with many hardships till he gets home.

Labour *to feel like a son of God* in every condition in which you are placed. Never forget you are on your Father's ground so long as you are here on earth. Never forget that a Father's hand sends all your mercies and crosses. Cast every care on Him. Be happy and cheerful in Him. Why indeed art thou ever sad if thou art the King's son? Why should men ever doubt, when they look at you, whether it is a pleasant thing to be one of God's children?

Labour *to behave towards others like a son of God*. Be blameless and harmless in your day and generation. Be a peacemaker among all you know. Seek for your children, sonship to God above everything else. Seek for them an inheritance in heaven, whatever else you do for them. No man leaves his children so well provided for as he who leaves them sons and heirs of God.

Persevere in your Christian calling, if you are a son of God, and press forward more and more. Be careful to lay aside every weight, and the sin which most easily besets you. Keep your eyes steadily fixed on Jesus. Abide in Him. Remember that without Him you can do nothing, and with Him you can do all things (John 15:5; Phil. 4:13). Watch and pray daily. Be steadfast, unmovable and always abounding in the work of the Lord. Settle it down in your heart, that not a cup of cold water, given in the name of a disciple, shall lose its reward, and that every year you are so much nearer home.

Yet a little time and he that shall come will come, and will not tarry. Then shall be the glorious liberty, and the full manifestation of the sons of God. Then shall the world acknowledge that they were the truly wise. Then shall the sons of God at length come of age. Then shall they no longer be heirs of expectancy, but heirs in possession. And then shall they hear with exceeding joy those comfortable words, 'Come, ye blessed of my Father, inherit the kingdom prepared for you from the foundation of the world' (Matt. 25:34). Surely that day will make amends for all!

That all who read this address may see the value of the inheritance of glory, and be found at length in possession of it, is my heart's desire and prayer.

Revelation 22:20

The Church has waited long
Her absent Lord to see;
And still in loneliness she waits,
A friendless stranger she.
Age after age has gone,
Sun after sun has set,
And still in weeds of widowhood
She weeps, a mourner yet.

Come, then, Lord Jesus, come!

Saint after saint on earth
Has liv'd, and lov'd, and died;
And as they left us one by one,
We laid them side by side:
We laid them down to sleep,
But not in hope forlorn;
We laid them but to ripen there,
Till the last glorious morn.

Come, then, Lord Jesus, come!

The serpent's brood increase,
The powers of hell grow bold,
The conflict thickens, faith is low,
And love is waxing cold.
How long, O Lord our God,
Holy and true and good,
Wilt Thou not judge Thy suffering Church,
Her sighs and tears and blood?

Come, then, Lord Jesus, come!

We long to hear Thy voice,
To see Thee face to face,
To share Thy crown and glory then,

As now we share Thy grace.
Should not the loving Bride
The absent Bridegroom mourn?
Should she not wear the weeds of grief
Until her Lord return?

Come, then, Lord Jesus, come!

The whole creation groans,
And waits to hear that voice
Which shall restore her comeliness,
And make her wastes rejoice.
Come, Lord, and wipe away
The curse, the sin, the stain,
And make this blighted world of ours
Thine own fair wold again.

Come, then, Lord Jesus, come!

Horatius Bonar

END NOTES

1. I am aware that Dean Alford does not take the view I have here stated. But his arguments do not satisfy me. My reasons will be found in my *Expository Thoughts on St Matthew*. Most of the foreign Reformers and English Puritans maintain, as I do, that the foolish virgins represent the unconverted.

2. 'Christ did never absolutely deny His having such a visible glorious kingdom upon earth as that which His disciples looked for; only He corrected their error as to the time of this kingdom appearing. Christ did not say to them that there never should be such restoration of the kingdom to Israel as their thoughts were running upon; only He telleth them the times and seasons were not for them to know; thereby acknowledging that such a kingdom should indeed be, as they did from the holy prophets expect. Herein was their error, not in expecting a glorious appearance of the kingdom of God, but in that they made account that this would be immediately.' *The Mysteries of Israel's Salvation* by Dr. Increase Mather, 1669, p. 130.

3. The reader who wishes to see this subject more fully discussed is strongly advised to read Horatius Bonar's *Prophetical Landmarks,* Andrew Bonar's *'Redemption Drawing Nigh',* Ogilvy's *Popular Objections to the Premillennial Advent Considered,* M'Neile on *the Second Advent*, and *On the Jews*, and Bickersteth on *Prophecy*. It is a matter for deep regret that no good commentary on Old Testament prophecy has yet been written. Keith on *Isaiah* is a step in the right direction. But a complete exposition of the Psalms and Prophets is yet wanting. The Lord grant that this gap in our theological literature may yet be filled up.

4. Preterism is the system of prophetical interpretation, held by those who consider the greater part of the prophecies in Revelation as fulfilled, and past already. Futurism is the system of those who consider the same prophecies to be as yet unfulfilled.

5. The substance of this Address was originally preached as the Annual Sermon on behalf of the London Society for promoting Christianity among the Jews, at the Rectory Church, Mary-le-bone, in May 1868.

6. 'The Symbolical or Hieroglyphical character is an art of communicating the conceptions of the mind by visible figures, which having metaphorical relation or similitude, or at least affinity to the conceptions, excite in others the same conceptions' – Daubuzon Revelation, p. 6, 1720.

'The Hieroglyphical characters are like all kinds of animals and members of men, and working tools, especially those of carpenters. For their writing does not show the discourse about the subject matter by the composition of syllables, but by the emphasis of the figures' – Diodorus Siculus, quoted by Daubuz, p. 8.

'From this way of writing arose a symbolical way of speaking too; the symbolical characters, which they were so conversant with, furnishing them continually with metaphors and others tropes, first in their mysterious or religious speeches and from them easily passing on to the vulgar matters. Which kind of speech set up the priests and wiser sort of men above the level of the vulgar, because such a figurative and florid kind of speech and notions seemed to add great beauty to their thoughts, and distinguished that of wise men from the plain style of the rest. Thence it comes that most of the Oriental languages, especially that of the poets, affect this way' – Daubuz, p. 8.

7. It is a curious fact that the fourth council of Toledo, held about the 640, made the following decree: 'Because there are many that do not receive the book of Apocalypse as authentic, and scorn to read it in the Church of God, if any one for the future shall refuse to receive it, or to read it in the Church, in the time of Mass, from Easter to Whitsuntide, he shall be excommunicated' – Cressener on Revelation, 1690.

8. 'Voltaire was pleased to say, that Sir Isaac Newton wrote his comment on the Revelation to console mankind for the great superiority he had over them in other respects. But Voltaire, though very agreeable, is yet a very superficial writer, and often mistaken in his judgment of men and things' – Bishop Newton on Prophecy, 1754.

9. 'Among the interpreters of Revelation in the last ages, there is scarce one of note who hath not made some discovery worth knowing' – Sir Isaac Newton on the Apocalypse, chapter 1, p. 253.

10. 'It is true, many things in the book of Revelation are obscure, and it is likely that the full clearing of them is not to be expected till God in some singular way shall open them up. Yet there are many clear, edifying and comfortable passages of God's mind in it, the Holy Ghost mixing them into be fed upon, to sweeten those passages that are more obscure, and to encourage the reader to search for the meaning of them' – Durham on Revelation, 1658.

11. Joseph Mede, the most learned and able interpreter of prophecy that this country can name among its divines, was remarkable for his modesty and humility. In a letter of his to Dr. Irviss, speaking of Apocalypse, chapter 14, he adds these words, 'I am by nature dilatory in all things, but in this let no man blame me if I take more pause than ordinary; for it has sunk deeply into my mind, that rashly to be the author of a false interpretation of Scripture is to take God's name in vain in a high degree' – Mede's Works, 1672.

12. A large part of this sermon is undoubtedly not of a prophetical character, but I feel that it may form a fitting conclusion to the whole volume, and therefore insert it unabridged.

13. The reader will of course understand that I am not speaking now of children who die in infancy, or of persons who live and die idiots.

DAY BY DAY WITH
J.C. RYLE

A NEW DAILY DEVOTIONAL
OF RYLE'S WRITINGS

EDITED BY | ERIC RUSSELL

Day by Day with Ryle

A new daily devotional of J. C. Ryle's writings

Eric Russell

J.C. Ryle has become one of the most-loved of British authors on church matters. He was the first Bishop of Liverpool, managing to establish a thriving diocese in that most sectarian of English cities. Although a convinced Evangelical he was regarded as fair-minded with those who disagreed with him.

His books have remained in print for a hundred years because Ryle was able to touch the person in the street with clear teaching on doctrinal matters. He showed how the Bible was *relevant*.

His writings thus lend themselves to a devotional format and here is a new selection different to any that have gone before. Here Eric Russell (Ryle's biographer) has arranged writings according to themes that develop the reader's understanding on a topic before moving on to new pastures.

It is as refreshing as it is profound.

ISBN 1-85792-959-4

REGENERATION

Being 'Born Again':
What it means and why it's necessary

J.C.RYLE

REGENERATION

Being 'Born Again': What it means and why it's necessary

J.C. Ryle

John Charles Ryle (1816 – 1900) was the first Bishop of Liverpool, England. He found himself faced with the difficult task of being an evangelical leader of a mixed diocese in the most sectarian of English cities. It was a recipe for strife, division and resentment, but throughout his period in office Ryle was respected by his colleagues to the extent that even one of his most strident opponents broke down and wept at the news of his death. He was able to master the difficult task of being firm in his beliefs and loving in his application of them. His gracious spirit is an example to us today.

In this powerful work, Ryle explains that divisive, often derided, (so often misapplied by advertising) term 'born again'. He explains what being 'born again' means, why it is necessary and how you can tell whether you are.

Much of the value of this publication, though, lies in what Ryle writes next. In his gracious yet firm way Ryle devotes the majority of the book to explaining how the objections people have had to the doctrine should be handled and overcome with gentle persuasion.

It is a supreme example of the art of persuasion, one that we all need to consider.

ISBN 1-85792-741-9

"Ryle's story told afresh by someone who understands it so well."
J. I. Packer

THAT MAN OF GRANITE
WITH THE HEART OF A CHILD

A NEW BIOGRAPHY OF
J.C. RYLE

ERIC RUSSELL

THAT MAN OF GRANITE WITH THE HEART OF A CHILD

A new biography of J.C. Ryle

Eric Russell

"It is very good to have Ryle's story told afresh by someone who understands it so well…Ryle was an Anglican to remember."

J. I. Packer

John Charles Ryle was born into a comfortable English family background - his father was a politician and businessman. Ryle was intelligent, a great sportsman (captain of cricket at Eton and Oxford) and was set for a career in his father's business, and then politics – a typical, well to do, 19th century family.

Then – disaster. The family awoke to find that their father's bank had failed, taking all the other businesses with it. Ryle had lost his job and his place in society. He resigned his commission in the local yeomanry and went to comfort his parents, brother and sisters. One moment a popular man with good prospects, the next the son of a bankrupt with no trade or profession.

Almost as a last resort, he was ordained into the ministry of the church. Who could have thought that such an uninspiring entry into the ministry could have such an impact on the spiritual life of a nation.

Ryle's reputation as a pastor and leader grew until he was appointed the first Bishop of Liverpool, a post he held for 20 years. He was an author who is still in print today (he put aside royalties to pay his father's debts) and a man once described by his successor as 'that man of granite with the heart of a child.' He changed the face of the English church.

Ryle stands as a colossus at the junction of two centuries – a hundred years after his death he still stands as an example to church leaders today of how to combine leadership, a firm faith and compassion.

Eric Russell was ordained as a Church of England minister but is better known as a college lecturer training teachers in Religious Studies. He has previously written about the history of the Liverpool diocese.

ISBN 1-85792-631-5

CHRISTIAN FOCUS PUBLICATIONS
publishes books for all ages

Our mission statement –

STAYING FAITHFUL

In dependence upon God we seek to help make His infallible Word, the Bible, relevant. Our aim is to ensure that the Lord Jesus Christ is presented as the only hope to obtain forgiveness of sin, live a useful life and look forward to heaven with Him.

REACHING OUT

Christ's last command requires us to reach out to our world with His gospel. We seek to help fulfill that by publishing books that point people towards Jesus and help them develop a Christ-like maturity. We aim to equip all levels of readers for life, work, ministry and mission.

Books in our adult range are published in three imprints.

Christian Focus contains popular works including biographies, commentaries, basic doctrine and Christian living. Our children's books are also published in this imprint.

Mentor focuses on books written at a level suitable for Bible College and seminary students, pastors, and other serious readers. The imprint includes commentaries, doctrinal studies, examination of current issues and church history.

Christian Heritage contains classic writings from the past.

Christian Focus Publications, Ltd
Geanies House, Fearn,
Ross-shire, IV20 1TW, Scotland, United Kingdom
info@christianfocus.com

For details of our titles visit us on our website
www.christianfocus.com